MARRIAGE In America

Understanding The Battle.
Outlining A Plan.

Grassfire

Printed in the United States of America
First Printing, 2015

ISBN 1-9391151-7-1

Grassfire
P.O. Box 277
Maxwell, IA 50161
www.Grassfire.com

Grassfire, a division of Grassroots Action, Inc., is a million-strong network of grassroots conservatives dedicated to equipping you with the tools that give you a real impact on the key issues of our day. We also operate a social networking site (Patriot Action.net) and a patriot-sourced news website (LibertyNews.com).

Table of Contents

We Don't Accept It!

During the first 2016 Republican presidential candidate debate, Ohio Governor John Kasich stated in just a few words why we are publishing this book.

Kasich's words came in response to a "gotcha" question from FOX News star and debate moderator Megyn Kelly loaded with jurisdictional confusion among the roles of the state, the church and family on the issue of same-sex marriage:

> KELLY: Governor Kasich, if you had a son or daughter who was gay or lesbian, how would you explain to them your opposition to same-sex marriage?[1]

Before we look at Kasich's answer, let's break down Kelly's question. As is typical for this issue, Kelly put Kasich on the defensive by making it personal: "If your son or daughter..." First off, Kasich has two daughters and no sons. Second, Kelly is asking a hypothetical which seems to have no basis in reality. Clearly, the implication of the question is that opposition to same-sex marriage is, at best, a heartless position that would be difficult to explain to a son or daughter.

Kasich is a governor of one of the most important states in presidential politics. He is the chief executive of over 50,000 employees. And yet, he was not asked the question from the vantage point of public policy. Kelly intentionally made this personal. She might as well have asked, "When did you stop beating your hypothetical gay son or daughter?"

It gets worse, because Kasich attempted to answer the question by further confusing the jurisdictions.

> KASICH: Well, look, I'm an old-fashioned person here, and I happen to believe in traditional marriage....

Interpretation — *I have these old, out-of-date values that I personally believe in, but...* With those words, Kasich relegated his position on same-sex marriage to a bygone era with little or no relevance to the current debate.

Then with his next few words, Kasich made the case for why we are publishing *Saving Marriage In America*. He continued:

> ...But I've also said the court has ruled... and we'll accept it.

The court has ruled... and we'll accept it?

According to Kasich (and sadly, most Americans in our day and time), the Supreme Court is not only the *final* arbiter of what the Constitution means, but the *only* arbiter of what the Constitution means. If the Supreme Court rules on an issue, our only option is to *accept it.*

End of story.

Or is it?

Saving Marriage In America makes a different case. The goal of this book is to help you see that what the Supreme Court did in June of 2015 was not the end of the debate on marriage in America. In fact, the court was wrong, plain and simple. This resource will show you how and why the five lawyers who wrote the majority opinion in the *Obergefell* case were wrong. We'll also help you sort through this issue from a perspective that doesn't leave you in a philosophical corner like John Kasich.

There is solid, constitutional ground upon which to stand and say that the Court was wrong in *Obergefell*, that the decision should be invalid and resisted, and that society should be built upon a preference for one-man, one-woman marriage. *Saving Marriage In America* rebuilds this foundation of truth. For example, did you know...

- The Constitution says *nothing* directly about marriage and the issue was left entirely to the states.

- Prior to 2001, no jurisdiction in recorded history accepted same-sex marriage. Almost every culture has affirmed man-woman marriage.

- Four Supreme Court justices said unequivocally that the Court's *Obergefell* decision was not only unconstitutional, but destructive to our very way of life.

- There is clear historical, cultural, societal and biblical reasoning for policies that defend natural marriage.

- While the Bible clearly illuminates this issue, there is no need to cite "chapter and verse" to build sound public policy supporting natural marriage.

- Every citizen's allegiance is to the Constitution, not a government and certainly not a court. And every citizen (not just Supreme Court justices) has a duty to protect and defend the Constitution.

How Saving Marriage Was Written

Saving *Marriage In America* covers these and other important aspects of this debate and is the collaborative work of Dr. Herb Titus and myself. I studied under Dr. Titus and have long admired his principled understanding of the Constitution. Shortly after the *Obergefell* decision, I approached Dr. Titus about helping me put together a principled response that would give citizens the proper historical and constitutional context for this issue. Dr. Titus provided the core constitutional and philosophical framework for what you see here. We then worked closely together to craft a final document that would give citizens a template for resisting this unconstitutional ruling and thereby helping save marriage in America. Finally, *Saving Marriage* includes the dissenting opinions in the *Obergefell* decision because these documents help provide a philosophical and legal roadmap for repairing the breach of *Obergefell.*

Gov. Kasich and others who believe that the Supreme Court has the *only* say in all things related to the Constitution are wrong. This error puts our entire society at risk. Our founding fathers would be greatly disturbed by the idea that we should "just accept" a ruling that is unconstitutional and destructive to our society.

It is my hope that after reading this resource, you will have the information you need to understand both *why* the Court's same-sex marriage is wrong and *how* it should be resisted as part of a plan to save marriage in America, and save our Republic.

Steve Elliott

August 2015

1.

How The Court Was Wrong

The five justices who issued the majority decision in the U.S. Supreme Court's homosexual marriage case (*Obergefell v. Hodges*) were wrong.

They were wrong morally.

They were wrong historically.

And they were wrong both legally and constitutionally.

The four dissenting justices did an admirable job explaining how the *Obergefell* decision is wrong constitutionally. We have included those historic and extremely important dissenting opinions in this work because the messages of Justices Roberts, Scalia, Thomas, and Alito are very important. If our society reverses the error of *Obergefell,* these dissenting opinions will be favorably remembered in the annals of history.

In summary, the dissenters establish very plainly that the Constitution says nothing of marriage. Nor is there any compelling reason to create a "due process" right because it is impossible to argue that same-sex marriage has been or is fundamental to our society or way of life. With some of the strongest language ever published in a Supreme Court decision, the dissenting justices called out the five-vote majority for a blatant act of lawless tyranny. According to Roberts, "five lawyers have closed the debate.... stealing this issue from the people... making dramatic social change." He adds:

> The majority's decision is an act of will, not legal judgment. The right it announces has no basis in the Constitution or the Court's precedent. The majority expressly disclaims judicial "caution" and omits even a pretense of humility, openly relying on its desire to remake society according to its own "new insight" in the "nature of injustice." As a result, the Court invalidates the marriage laws of more than half the States and orders the transformation of a social institution that has formed the basis of human society for millennia, for the Kalahari bushmen and the Han Chinese, the Carthaginians and the Aztecs. Just who do we think we are?

Although it was difficult to do, Justice Scalia was even more scathing in his rebuke of his fellow justices, calling the majority opinion a "threat to democracy" under a "thin veneer of law," and stating:

> Today's decree says that my Ruler, and the Ruler of 320 million Americans coast-to-coast, is a majority of the nine lawyers on the Supreme Court.... This

> is a naked judicial claim to legislative — indeed, super-legislative — power; a claim fundamentally at odds with our system of government."

Scalia then said any such government run by nine lawyers "does not deserve to be called a democracy" and compared the unconstitutional actions of five justices to a "judicial Putsch" — a not-so-subtle reference to Adolph Hitler's illegal efforts to overthrow a legitimate German government. When a Supreme Court justice calls the actions of his colleagues a "Putsch" while the Chief Justice equates it to "stealing" with "no basis in the Constitution or this Court's precedent," no citizen should feel a duty to blindly submit to the Court's ruling!

Inventing A Right To Same-Sex Marriage

With no real constitutional grounds to stand on, Justice Anthony Kennedy — writing for the majority — was forced to bend reason, ignore history and abandon even basic principles of constitutional law to construe a constitutional "right" for two persons of the same sex to marry. The error of Kennedy's ways can be seen from the opening statement to the concluding paragraph. In fact, Kennedy's argument does not even pretend to be a judicial one applying the law to the facts. Rather, from beginning to end, Justice Kennedy embarks on a psychological/religious quest to prove that:

> "The Constitution promises liberty to all within its reach, a liberty that includes certain specific rights that allow persons ... to define and express their identity ... by marrying someone of the same sex and having their marriages deemed lawful on the same terms and conditions as marriages between persons of the opposite sex."

Thus after decades of meandering through the "penumbras" of the Constitution to unearth never before discovered "rights," the justices have arrived at the "holy grail" of modern liberty — the right to "define and express [one's] identity."

First, Justice Kennedy addresses the question of why would anyone in his right mind want to find their "identity" in an opposite sex relationship to which they do not aspire? Readily, Justice Kennedy discovers the answer. After consulting the annals of human history, he finds the "transcendent importance of marriage," which "always has promised **nobility and dignity**," "**sacred** to those who live by their religions," "**unique**[**ly**] **fulfill**[**ing**] to those who find meaning in the secular realm," "a life that ... becomes **greater than just the two persons**," and **essential** to our most profound **hopes and aspirations**." (emphasis added)

Second, Justice Kennedy addresses the question: Why would anyone in his right mind deny to same-sex couples all these wonderful benefits so long enjoyed by opposite sex couples? Again, Justice Kennedy has the ready answer: "the petitioners seek [marriage] for themselves because of their **respect** – and **need** – for its privileges and responsibilities." Indeed, Justice Kennedy finds their need overwhelming: "their **immutable nature dictates** that same-sex marriage is their **only real path** to this profound commitment." (emphasis added) Indeed, it would be especially cruel to deny the three same-sex couples access to marriage, two of which "fell in love" with each other, and the other of which have adopted special needs children.

Third, although the three same-sex couples are especially worthy and needy, Justice Kennedy cannot avoid the question how to accommodate them "within the lawful realm" of accepted behavior. Conveniently, he finds the history of marriage to be "one of both continuity and change," and that "even as confined to opposite-sex relations" the "institution – has evolved overtime." Further, not only have there been such micro-evolutionary changes but, Justice Kennedy observed that there have been macro-evolutionary changes wherein "same-sex intimacy" has been elevated in personal "dignity," no longer condemned by law and society. Thus, Justice Kennedy concluded:

> These new insights have strengthened, not weakened, the institution of marriage. Indeed, changed understandings of marriage are characteristic of a Nation where new dimensions of freedom become apparent to new generations....

Capping this new understanding of freedom, Justice Kennedy recounted that in 1973 the

American Psychiatric Association led the way to what "in more recent years [when] psychiatrists and others recognized that sexual orientation is both a **normal** expression of human sexuality and **immutable**."

Loosed from a past history of intolerance, and newly launched on a sea of change, Justice Kennedy's quest for the Holy Grail of liberty comes to a climax in a final paragraph:

> No union is more profound than marriage, for it embodies the highest ideals of love, fidelity, devotion, sacrifice, and family. In forming a marital union, two people become something greater than they once were. As some of the petitioners in these cases demonstrate, marriage embodies a love that may endure even past death.... Their hope is not to be condemned to live in loneliness, excluded from one of civilization's oldest institutions. They ask for equal dignity in the eyes of the law. The Constitution grants them that right.

Court-Ingrained Reality

Throughout his opinion, Justice Kennedy does not find "facts." Rather, he creates them whenever it suits his immediate purpose. When confronted with the view that "marriage ... by its nature [is] a gender-differentiated union of man and woman," Justice Kennedy chooses not to answer. Instead, he bypasses the question, stating that such a view is held "in good faith by reasonable and sincere people here and throughout the world." In contrast, when asked whether, by their lawsuit, the petitioning same-sex couples "inten[ded] to "demean the revered idea and reality of marriage," Justice Kennedy jumped right in, saying unequivocally "that is neither their purpose, nor their submission," and reassuring, "[to] the contrary, it is the enduring importance of marriage that underlies the petitioners' contentions."

Missing from this discussion is any hint that the drive for same-sex marriage has been to destroy marriage altogether even though as early as 2012 there were voices in the LBGT community that the push for gay marriage was not about the right to marry, but the eventual destruction of marriage and the "traditional family." Instead, Justice Kennedy filled three full paragraphs of his opinion with romantic descriptions of the three same-sex couples' "love" and "commitment," to the end that "[t]heir **stories** reveal that they seek not to denigrate marriage but rather to live their lives, or honor their spouses' memory, joined by its bond."

In keeping with this sympathetic theme towards the petitioning couples, Justice Kennedy twice empathized, asserting that they could not really help themselves to find their personal identity in a same-sex marriage, as contrasted with an opposite-sex marriage. According to Justice Kennedy a same-sex marriage was the same-sex couples' **only** path to their profound commitment to the "respect – and need – for the privileges and responsibilities of marriage because their "**immutable nature dictates**" it. That immutable nature is later identified by Justice Kennedy as their "**sexual orientation.**" In other words, Justice Kennedy opined that these three petitioning couples had no choice. Because of their innate orientation to other persons of the same sex, they would not have access to traditional marriage. What could be a greater barrier to the constitutional promises of liberty than that?

According to Justice Kennedy, sexual orientation is "immutable" because some "psychologists and others" recognize it to be so, citing the *amicus brief* of the American Psychological Association. But the American Psychological Association website reads, as follows:

> There is no consensus among scientists about the exact reasons that an individual develops a heterosexual, bisexual, gay, or lesbian orientation. Although much research has examined the possible genetic, hormonal, developmental, social and cultural influences on sexual orientation, no findings have emerged that permit scientists to conclude that sexual orientation is determined by any particular factor or factors. Many think that nature and nurture both play complex roles; most people experience little or no sense of choice about their sexual orientation.[2]

Additionally, the American Psychological Association website states that, notwithstanding one's sexual orientation, a person still has a choice whether to act on that orientation.[3] Further, some studies indicate that gay men and lesbian women can become heterosexual in both orientation and behavior – if they want to.

Kennedy ignores even the conclusions of the APA and hangs his argument on his "immutable" theory. If same-sex couples have no choice, then, of course, we cannot deny them marriage or we will abandon them on an "island" of loneliness and despair in which they will never be able to attain their sacred right to identity!

Immutable... and Good!

Throughout his opinion, Justice Kennedy spoke of same-sex marriage in glowing and affirming terms. Just like opposite-sex couples, same-sex couples would find "dignity" and "nobility" if provided equal access to marry. Such equal access would, Justice Kennedy proclaimed, satisfy the same-sex couples' "most profound hopes and aspirations." Indeed, if only such couples could get married, they would "find other freedoms, such as expression, intimacy, and spirituality."

As for any alleged "harmful outcomes" put forth by those in opposition to same-sex marriage, Justice Kennedy replied that "these cases involve only the right of two consenting adults whose marriage would pose **no risk of harm to themselves or third parties**." Kennedy's words were not the result of the issue of "harmful outcomes" being thoroughly examined by the Supreme Court or the courts below.

Rather, Justice Kennedy observed, the states of Michigan, Ohio, Kentucky and Tennessee failed to establish any "foundation" upon which to prove their harmful concerns. One of those states, Michigan, had attempted to offer expert testimony in support of those concerns but had been prevented from doing so. So the cases came to the United States Supreme Court without any real record of possible "harmful outcomes" of encouraging and facilitating same-sex activities. And the Court took full advantage of this omission, deliberately ignoring the realities of the homosexual lifestyle that, if attended to, would have destroyed their romanticization of homoerotic relationships.

In a last ditch effort to bring this reality into the case before the Supreme Court, the United States Justice Foundation prepared a Petition for a Rehearing, submitting it to the State of Michigan for filing in the Supreme Court. But the State of Michigan declined. Had the petition been filed, it would have presented to the Court documented evidence of numerous serious health risks directly resulting from homosexual behavior, even in those countries that have endorsed same-sex marriage.[4] Attached to the Petition were 23 proffers of expert testimony concerning the health risks to those who participate in same-sex activities and to others, the health risks that Justice Kennedy did not find in the judicially-sanitized record, including but not limited to:

- Disproportionately same-sex coupling invites the Human Immunodeficiency

Virus ("HIV") weakening the immune system of men engaged in same-sex activity which is already at epidemic proportions and increasing.

- Antiviral therapy has practically transformed HIV from an acute fatal illness to a chronic disease, extending life to HIV sufferers who receive costly drugs at taxpayers expense, while remaining sexually active continuing the transmission of HIV to others and the development of other sexually transmitted diseases.

- Notwithstanding the extension of life enjoyed by HIV sufferers, studies still show that rates of morbidity of homosexual males, even those who are married, are higher than for heterosexual males. At the same time because active homosexuals are disproportionately disease prone, there is a consequent disproportionate share of federal disease research dollars.

- Sexually transmitted diseases generally are disproportionately suffered at higher rates in the homosexual population, which is due in part to the unnatural types of sex practiced, the anus not being conducive to repeated penetration, whereas the vagina, by contrast, is self-lubricating, and more resistant to infectious organisms than the rectum or colon.

- Homosexuals are disproportionately sexually promiscuous, contributing to the spread of venereal disease, even in those countries that recognize same-sex marriages, where "open" marriages are the norm.

- Subsets of the gay population engage in anonymous sex, including HIV positive men seeking out men to infect with the HIV virus as an added thrill.

- Even in those cultures where homosexual coupling is more openly tolerated, homosexuality is associated with a higher prevalence of psychiatric disorders, including suicide, than in the heterosexual community.

- In disproportionate numbers both homosexual men and Lesbian women account for the sexual molestation of children, although comprising only a relatively small percentage of the general population (about 1.6 to 3 percent) they molest about half of all sexually victimized children. Gays are not only more likely to molest children, they are more likely to molest many more children before being caught and convicted.

- Homosexuality is disproportionately linked to other pathologies and deviant behaviors, such as sadomasochism. [5]

This evidence never reached the eyes or ears of the justices — evidence they undoubtedly were glad to ignore.

Recuse Thyself!

Beyond the moral arguments and the legal arguments and the constitutional arguments, a very strong case can be made that at least two of the five justices who made this monumental decision for 320 million Americans should never have had a vote in the case!

Months before the same-sex marriage cases were placed on the Supreme Court docket, two justices, Ruth Bader Ginsburg and Elena Kagan, let it be known that they personally favored same-sex marriage. More than that, knowing full well that the same-sex marriage issue would ultimately reach the Court for decision, both justices – one in 2014 and the other in 2015 - officiated at a same-sex wedding. Justice Ginsburg went even further, giving a press interview in which she said that it "would not take a large adjustment" for the American people to accept homosexual marriage:

> The change in people's attitude on that issue has been enormous. In recent years, people have said, 'This is the way I am.' And others looked around, and we discovered it's our next door neighbor - we're very fond of them. Or it's our child's best friend, or even our child. I think that as more and more people came out and said that 'this is who I am,' the rest of us recognized that they are one of us.[6]

Then, just weeks after the oral argument and while the case was in the bosom of the Court,

Justice Ginsburg again officiated at a same-sex marriage – by the powers vested in her by the "Constitution" of the United States, with a sly emphasis on "Constitution."

All of this was placed before the Supreme Court of the United States by the Foundation for Moral Law which filed a friend-of-the-court motion calling for Justices Ginsburg and Kagan to "recuse" themselves from the case. In support of the motion, the Foundation reminded the two justices that two canons of judicial ethics mandated that they not participate in the decision. First, a judge should not "make public comment on the merits of the matter pending ... in any court." Second, a judge must "act at all times in a manner that promotes public confidence in the integrity and impartiality of the judiciary." Additionally, the Foundation rested its recusal motion on a federal statute that requires any federal judge to "disqualify himself in any proceeding in which his impartiality might reasonably be questioned."

Although the Foundation's motion was dated April 27, 2015, it did not appear on the Supreme Court's formal docket until after June 17, just nine days before the same-sex marriage case decision was announced. Even then the motion did not appear as a "motion," but the clerk of the court denominated it to be a "request."[7] Not surprisingly, there is nothing on the Supreme Court's docket sheet indicating that the motion was ever submitted to either Justice Ginsburg or Justice Kagan, much less ever acted upon.

Thus, even the validity of one of the most disruptive and controversial decisions ever issued by this Court is cloaked in questions and mystery. The truth of what happened to this critical "recusal" brief and whether the justices ever reviewed the motion is still shrouded in the "penumbras" of the *Obergefell* decision. It is a secret, and most likely will remain a secret, hidden from the American people, even though the votes of both justices were absolutely necessary to the outcome of this extraordinary case wherein five unelected justices imposed upon the People their personal views that the Constitution – which says nothing whatsoever about marriage – requires every State in the union to honor same-sex unions as a lawful marriage.

Despite the obvious errors of the ruling, its lack of constitutional grounds, its betrayal of history, and its invention of rights, as Justice Roberts noted, we have a decision that "invalidates the marriage laws of more than half the States and orders the transformation of a social institution that has formed the basis of human society for millennia." Where do we go from here? Can the institution of marriage in America be saved, and if so, where do we begin? To find out, we must go back to the very beginnings.

2.

Overruling God And Creating An Idol

Justice Kennedy lives in a depressingly sad universe. At least that's what we can conclude from his majority opinion in the *Obergefell* same-sex marriage case. Kennedy's world is so sad and lonely that he and four of his colleagues felt compelled to create a brand new constitutional right — one never before recognized in human history prior to the recent blip of the past 15 years.

In addition to Kennedy's world being sad, it is atheistic to its core. Not only is God not acknowledged by name, but Justice Kennedy leaves (i) no space for God, as Creator, to rule, (ii) no role for God, as Judge to punish, and (iii) no hope from God as Redeemer, to save. According to Justice Kennedy's godless worldview, it is a lonely universe that man occupies and he needs all the help that he can get if he is to survive. In words that sound more religious than legal, Kennedy very much frames his argument around his idea that "marriage responds to the universal fear that a lonely person might call out only to find no one there." Isn't this, at its essence, the reason people across millennia have sought to interpret their lives through faith in a transcendent reality, i.e. God? The late Francis Schaeffer framed this discussion for an entire generation with his book, *He Is There And He Is Not Silent*. Yet what we see in Kennedy's decision and thinking is the end result of pursuing religious impulses in a strictly secular model. There is no God in Kennedy's legal world and thus all he can see is a group of people who will be "condemned to live in loneliness" if he doesn't act. So the atheistic Kennedy becomes... god, and creates *"ex nihilo"* (out of nothing) a new right!

But, as Justice Thomas writes in dissent, the same-sex majority's lonely atheistic vision of the human condition is not that of America's founders. Having "proclaimed in the Declaration of Independence that 'all men are created equal' and 'endowed by their Creator with certain unalienable rights,'" the American "vision of mankind [was one] in which all humans are created in the image of God and therefore of inherent worth." Thus, Justice Thomas concluded, that "human dignity has long been understood in this country to be innate," and beyond the power of any human institution, including the United States Supreme Court, to bestow or to restore.

Ignoring the Natural Order

Justice Kennedy views the power, and thus the role, of the Supreme Court through an entirely different lens. Instead of acknowledging God as the one who has conferred our rights, and therefore, who alone defines those rights, Justice Kennedy believes that the Court is empowered to extend the unalienable right of liberty to three same-sex couples who "seek to find that liberty by marrying someone of the same sex and having their marriages deemed lawful on the same terms and conditions as marriages between persons of the opposite sex." And he assumes that by granting same-sex couples that right the Supreme Court has set them free.

Kennedy's world is so harshly atheistic that he would not even take a pure "law of nature" approach to this question and review the issue beyond any biblical or religious reference in strict terms of what can be called natural revelation. Regarding sexual relations, this is what we used to call "the birds and the bees" and it is the basic truth of heterosexuality that is evident in every animal in creation. It is so plain that for most children, the first words they can speak ("mama" and "dada") demonstrate the human brain's ability to make profound distinctions in human sexuality.

All of human history acknowledges this "natural law" perspective of marriage. As Justice Roberts noted, even the petitioners in the case arguing for same-sex marriage conceded "that they are not aware of any society that permitted same-sex marriage before 2001" and such recognition in the U.S. did not occur until 2003. History and the obvious law of nature had to be ignored and dismissed by Kennedy and his team of social movers.

God's Design Not Human Needs

One thing is certain. We know that Justice Kennedy and his four concurring colleagues do not – indeed, cannot – believe that God specially created the institution of marriage, either as natural order of things revealed in nature or as revealed in the first two chapters of the Old Testament book of Genesis, and as confirmed by Jesus Christ in the New Testament book of Matthew. As Jesus summarized the law of marriage, it has been and will always be thus:

> "Have you not read that he who made them from the beginning made them male and female, and said, 'For this reason as man shall leave his father and mother and be joined to his wife, and the two shall become one flesh'? What therefore God has joined together, let not man put asunder."

Eschewing these immortal words of God from the Holy Scriptures, nevertheless, Justice Kennedy acknowledges that two essential features of marriage are that, from the beginning, (i) it has been a "lifelong union of a man and a woman," and that (ii) it "allows two people to find a life that could not be found alone, for a marriage becomes greater than just the two persons." But Justice Kennedy assiduously avoids attributing marriage as a relationship deliberately designed by God in response to what God determined that man especially needed. According to Genesis 2, the man, Adam, specially needed a "help meet." And God supplied that by fashioning the woman, Eve, to meet that need.

And, then, God established the institution of marriage through which not only Adam and Eve might meet each others need, but that all human males and females would do in like manner in the future. Marriage, then, was created by God as an exclusive relationship specially designed for Adam and Eve and all future generations.

Justice Kennedy, however, has other ideas, attributing marriage to have arisen sphinx-like "from the most basic human needs," and thus, recognized as "essential to our most profound hopes and aspirations." Not only do Justice Kennedy and his colleagues not subscribe to the Biblical account of God's origination of marriage, but they go to great lengths to distance their historical account from that of the Holy Scriptures. In support of their conclusion that marriage is central "to the human condition" existing for "millennia," the majority of justices cite Confucius, rather than Moses. Instead of citing the Apostle Paul's teaching on the family, they tap into Cicero. Finally, Justice Kennedy buries the Judeo/Christian history of marriage in a multi-cultural smorgasbord of unnamed "religious and philosophical texts" celebrating the "beauty of marriage."

To what end does the Court substitute this naturalistic origin for marriage for the divine revelation in Genesis? The answer is that Justice Kennedy must discredit the idea that marriage is a "timeless institution" – fixed, uniform and universal – and thus forever inaccessible to "two persons of the same sex." By attributing the rise of marriage to "human needs," undefined by God, the same-sex majority justices set themselves free to assess anew whether there has been a change in human needs that would justify redefining marriage so as to include same-sex couples.

First, Justice Kennedy begins with the particular needs of the three same-sex couples in the case before the Court who are seeking marriage "for themselves" because of their personal "needs ... for its privileges and responsibilities." For Petitioner James Obergefell and his now deceased partner, John Arthur, the Court deemed that Mr. Obergefell's desire to have Mr. Arthur "listed as the surviving spouse on Mr. Arthur's death certificate," was a relevant and sufficient need. As for Petitioners April DeBoer and Jayne Rowse, the Court concluded that they had a need to be free "from the continuing uncertainty" that their unmarried status created with respect to three adopted children. Finally, petitioners Ijpe DeKoe and Thomas Kostura were found to have a need to have Tennessee, their chosen place of residence, recognize their New York marriage.

Second, the Court catalogues a range of "human needs" – from "identity," to "nobility," to "dignity," to "autonomy," to "intimacy," to "destiny," to "security," to "safety," and to "spirituality" — that are available if these same-sex couples and others are allowed to marry, but denied if they are excluded from marriage. Thus, untethered from God's singular, identified need of one man for one woman united in covenant union as husband and wife, the Court remade marriage in its own image, extending beyond God's creation, and blessing them male and male, and female and female.

The Procreative Purpose Of Marriage

Having re-invented marriage to respond to the human condition, the Court then re-invents the purpose of marriage. Marriage is, Justice Kennedy explains, of "transcendent importance" because it is "essential to our most profound hopes and aspirations." The freedom to marry, he continues, opens the door to personal "expression, intimacy and spirituality." Indeed, Justice Kennedy says, marriage, as "a keystone of our social order ... embodies the highest ideals of love, fidelity, devotion, sacrifice, and family." Marriage, he concludes, "offers unique fulfillment to those who find meaning in the secular realm."

Having concluded that marriage arose out of human needs, it is not surprising to hear from Justice Kennedy that the purpose of marriage is to meet those human needs. Once again, because Justice Kennedy ignores the Biblical account of man's origin, he is mistaken about the divine, and therefore, the overriding purpose of marriage and the family — to exercise dominion over God's creation, not as Justice Kennedy assumes, to meet man's deepest needs.

Genesis 1:26-28 reads as follows:

And God said, Let us make man in our image, after our likeness: and let them have

> *dominion.... So God created man in his own image, in the image of God created he him: male and female created he them. And God blessed them, and God said unto them, be fruitful and multiply, and replenish the earth, and subdue it: and have dominion over the fish of the sea, and over the fowl of the air, and over every living thing that moveth upon the earth.*

Picture oneself as Adam or Eve in the Garden of Eden. What would be one's response to this enormous assignment? Immediately, one would recognize that the job was too big for two people no matter how committed one to another, and no matter how fitting Eve was designed to be Adam's helpmate. Only through having children could they have possibly envisioned compliance with God's command.

Flashing forward to Noah and his family after the flood had devastated the entire earth, we learn that once again God commanded, this time to Noah and his three sons: "Be fruitful and multiply, and fill the earth." No matter how daunting the task, Genesis 10 attests that Noah's three sons and their generations populated the earth family by family. But, according to Genesis 11, not without a fight at the Tower of Babel, where God scattered the people all over the earth, quelling their rebellion against the dominion mandate.

After Babel, this procreative purpose of the marriage relationship was traced from Noah's sons through Abraham, Isaac and Jacob, when it was again challenged by the Egyptian Pharaoh, who ordered the death of all male Jewish boys. Under Moses, and then Joshua, it was restored to God's people who, once they reached the promised land, received the land, divided up family by family. This family free enterprise system is confirmed as normative by both the New, as well as the Old Testaments. God's people are commanded to work. Husbands are exhorted to provide for their families, wives are commended for supplying necessaries, and parents are urged to lay up an inheritance for their children.

By the time of America's founding it was well established that God had authorized man — family by family — to exercise dominion, out of which came the unalienable right to private property. The great English legal scholar, Sir William Blackstone, traced the common law of private property back to Genesis, reciting its origin in the Biblical dominion mandate, and expressly excluding all other historical accounts of property ownership. The early American State Constitutions secured to the people "certain inherent rights, of which, they cannot "deprive or divest their posterity; namely, the enjoyment of life, and liberty, with the means of acquiring and possessing property...."

Such an inherent right cannot be secure if the family order becomes dependent upon persons or organizations outside the family. God has established the one-male, one-female union legally, biologically, morally and spiritually as the only one capable of carrying out the Biblical mandate to procreate. Although a male/male or female/female couple may raise children, they cannot conceive children without outside help. Such inherent dependency reveals that a same-sex couple cannot function as a procreative unit independent from the State. Only a man and a woman in a covenant union as husband and wife can serve as a buffer against the power of the State, and carry forward the dominion purpose of God.

Kennedy's Marriage Idol

According to Justice Kennedy's picture of marriage, as long as same-sex couples are excluded from marriage, they cannot be truly free. Liberty, he claims, extends to same-sex couples only if they may choose marriage. Justice Kennedy asserts that having the right to choose marriage is "central to individual dignity and autonomy, including intimate choices that define personal identity and beliefs." Indeed, Justice Kennedy insists, "[t]he nature of marriage is that, through its enduring bond, two persons together can find other freedoms, such as expression, intimacy, and spirituality.' Marriage, Justice Kennedy opines, "supports a two-person union unlike any other in its importance to the committed individuals."

Marriage then for same-sex couples is an altar call. And while it may only have saving power in the "secular realm," nevertheless, the Court has ministered to all those who are heavy-laden. The State is here. What is it that you want? Liberty you say? By marrying someone of the same sex? The law of marriage no longer stands in the way.

The Supreme Court has ordained us, making it possible to confer upon you all the benefits that two people of the opposite sex who love one another have had "for millenia and across civilizations." For the Court has said:

> [S]ame sex couples may exercise the fundamental right to marry. No longer may this liberty be denied to them. [T]he State laws challenged by the Petitioners in these cases are now held invalid to the extent that they exclude same-sex couples from civil marriage on the same terms and conditions as opposite sex couples.

And the Court saw that it was good.

And in the process overruled God.

So it was. On June 26, in the year of our Lord 2015, and in the two hundred thirty-ninth year of our nation's independence, the Supreme Court set the nation free from the laws of nature and of nature's God, overruling our founder's declaration that we are created by God, and are ruled by God who not only created us, but endowed us with our unalienable rights of life, liberty and the pursuit of happiness.

3.

A Plan To Save Marriage In America

On June 26, 2015, the United States Supreme Court "legalized" same-sex marriage in the United States of America. Or so we have been told.

Is this true? Is it possible that with the stroke of a pen, a bare majority of five justices out of nine made legal what had been for almost all of human history and American history illegal? Apparently so — if you believe what most State Governors and Attorneys General have said. "We must obey," they say. The "rule of law" demands it, they cry. Their "oath of office" commands it, they declare.

Politicians will offer sound bites of resistance but most will have nothing to say after beating their chests about how inappropriate the ruling is. At the end of the day, most of our elected officials share the prevailing view that what the Supreme Courts says is the *law of the land*. Plain and simple. Resistance is futile.

We the People are told that we, too, must agree — two people of the same sex are just as entitled to marry, and enjoy all the benefits of marriage, as two people of the opposite sex.

Thus, we are instructed, same-sex marriage is now the law of the land, not as a result of a vote by the people or our representatives but by the pen of five lawyers. Just roll over like a submissive puppy and accept the edict.

However, just the opposite is the true story. But it's a story few want, or are willing, to even contemplate, which is why we're telling it here. So let's get started with Step One...

Step One: It's Our Oath!

The truth is, each elected and appointed government official and civil servant *in fact* has a sworn duty to ensure that the Constitution is upheld — that we are ruled by laws and not by men. The U.S. Code states plainly the oath required of all (except the President) in "elected or appointed to an office of honor or profit in the civil service or uniformed services":

> I, ________, do solemnly swear (or affirm) that I will support and defend the Constitution of the United States against all enemies, foreign and domestic; that I will bear true faith and allegiance to the same; that I take this obligation freely, without any mental reservation or purpose of evasion; and that I will well and faithfully discharge the duties of the office on which I am about to enter. So help me God."[8]

Likewise, naturalized citizens must swear (or affirm) an oath that includes the same direct affirmation of allegiance to the Constitution. Even reading the naturalization oath is revealing as to the true essence of what our nation actually is. First, foreigners must renounce any other allegiances:

> *"I hereby declare, on oath, that I absolutely and entirely renounce and abjure all allegiance and fidelity to any foreign prince, potentate, state, or sovereignty, of whom or which I have heretofore been a subject or citizen..."*

Foreigners wishing to become citizens must "*absolutely and entirely renounce*" any allegiance to a foreign ruler or state. And then what are new citizens declaring their allegiance to? The "United States"? Our "government"? Our "president and elected officials"? Absolutely not. Unlike British "subjects" who announced their allegiance to "Her Majesty Queen Elizabeth, her heirs and successors", Americans swear no allegiance to a man (or woman) or even a government. We swear to the *Constitution!* Here is the full beginning of the naturalization oath:

> *I hereby declare, on oath, that I absolutely and entirely renounce and abjure all allegiance and fidelity to any foreign prince, potentate, state, or sovereignty, of whom or which I have heretofore been a subject or citizen; that I will support and defend the Constitution and laws of the United States of America against all enemies, foreign and domestic; that I will bear true faith and allegiance to the same;* [9]

So Step One in the resistance to an unconstitutional Supreme Court ruling is to understand our oath and to affirm and embrace our responsibility as citizens to uphold the Constitution. This isn't simply some politician's heavy weight to bear. We The People bear the burden of supporting and defending the Constitution. In the case of the *Obergefell* marriage ruling, we have four justices who have openly called this decision judicial tyranny. Roberts, Scalia et.al. are all-but rhetorically begging citizens to rise up and embrace their duty to defend the Constitution.

It begins with you and me. We must affirm our duty to uphold the Constitution, a concept upon which our nation was founded yet is all-but forgotten in our day and time.[10] One way to re-establish our duty as citizens to the Constitution would be to require every native-born American at an appropriate time to take the same oath that a naturalized citizen takes.

Step One is to reclaim *your oath* to defend the Constitution. Saving marriage isn't about someone else doing something. First and foremost, it is about We The People — first individually and then as a community action — reclaiming the weighty duty of defending the Constitution. That's Step One. Then, we must know clearly that the Supreme Court has broken faith with the Constitution.

Step Two: Declare The Ruling Contrary To Nature

The idea that a court opinion, even that of the highest court in the land, can change the definition of marriage is predicated on the unproved (and unprovable) assumption that marriage, its legal obligations and privileges, was invented by men. Marriage wasn't invented by men. Rather, marriage is part of both the "general revelation" or the natural order (law of nature) and the "special revelation" of the Holy Scriptures (both Old and New Testaments). Marriage is created by God:

> *Have you not read that he who made them from the very beginning male and female, and said, "For this reason a man shall leave his father and mother and be joined to his wife, and the two shall become one flesh"? So they are no longer two but one flesh.* [Matthew 19:4-6(a).]

And governed by the laws of God. Matthew 19:6(b)-9. Until very recently in our nation's history, discussing a Bible verse in the context of public policy was generally accepted and not highly scorned.[11] Today, quoting a Bible verse in a public setting to establish or defend marriage will raise loud objections and accusations of religious intolerance and bigotry.

But the God-given law of marriage is so fundamental that it is evident for all to see. Man-woman marriage is *natural* and everything else is *unnatural*, or against nature. In fact, the "natural" nature of marriage is reflected in the respective physiology of the human male and female. Indeed, the differences between the designs of the reproductive and gastroenterology systems inform us that the male anatomy is not conducive to repeated penetration, while the female anatomy is self-lubricating and allowing smoother penetration.

The heterosexual nature of marriage is fundamental to what marriage is. According to common law, a marriage was not complete until it was consummated "with bodily knowledge," as the great Sir William Blackstone wrote in his Commentaries on the Laws of England. And according to the law of nature, consummation requires the matching of complementary parts of men and women. While this conjoining of opposite sexes can occur without the creation of a new child, same-sex sexual activity is always barren. As the writer of the book of Ecclesiastes has observed, "Consider the work of God; who can make straight what he has made crooked?" Eccl. 7:13. Marriage, like, gravity, is something for man to discover, but impossible for man to change.

In summary, even if the Supreme Court voted unanimously that a same-sex couple has a legal right to marry, that ruling would not make it so because, according to what is plainly made known to all people across all times ("the laws of nature and of nature's God"), it is simply factually and legally impossible for any union of two persons of the same sex to be married. The difference between "mama" and "dada" is one of the first things that infants can articulate. We see the natural order all around us. Nearly all of human history except the brief blip of the past two or so decades has acknowledged the natural male-female order. And while we receive great affirmation from the Bible as to the origin of and purpose for marriage, man-woman marriage is plain for everyone to see in every aspect of the natural order.

So Step Two is to unashamedly declare that — across all cultures and religions and governments — man-woman marriage is the natural order. Everything else is unnatural. Stand securely on this ground. Don't give in. Cite the facts of the lack of any historical legal support for same-sex marriage prior to 2001. Call a spade a spade.

Step Three: Reject Judicial Supremacy

Next in our plan of resistance to an unconstitutional Supreme Court ruling is to reject the idea of "judicial supremacy."[12] Most Americans today believe that the Supreme Court decides what the Constitution says and determines what the Constitution actually means, and therefore must be blindly obeyed. Our forebears would be horrified by this concept. They would say we exchanged the tyranny of a king (England) for the tyranny of five kings (Supreme Court).

We lost our way in recent decades as the sound idea of "judicial review" has expanded into the judicial supremacy or tyranny we see today. "It is emphatically the province and duty of the judicial department to say what the law is." Every lawyer in America has read this sentence taken from the most-cited case in American legal history — *Marbury v. Madison*. Penned by the great Chief Justice John Marshall in 1803, it is commonly misread to mean that whatever a majority of justices on the Supreme Court says, is what the law is. Nothing could be further than the truth. Twice, Justice Marshall stated — both because of his oath to support the Constitution and because of the Constitution, itself, expressly states "this Constitution is the supreme law of the land" — the law of the Constitution and the Court's opinion of that law is not one and the same thing.

John Marshall did not make this up. Rather, he simply was walking in the footsteps of two prominent jurists who preceded him — the venerable Moses and the great Blackstone. In an effort to understand our Constitution, we must understand the great sources which inspired our system of government. Before God gave Moses the Ten Commandments, written by the finger of God's own hand, God appointed Moses as the first judge of Israel. Exodus 18:13. As judge, Moses explained, he resolved disputes "between one and another" by "mak[ing] them know the statutes of God and his laws." In other words, Moses did not make up the law. Rather, he discovered the law and, then after finding the facts, applied the law to those facts. 3300 years later, Blackstone would similarly write that judges are the "depositary of the law; the living oracles ... who are bound by an oath to decide according to the law of the land," that is, " not ... according to his own private judgment, but according to the known laws...; not delegated to pronounce a new law, but to maintain and expound the old one." As Chief Justice Marshall observed, "Courts are mere instruments of law, and can will nothing.... Judicial power is never exercised for the purpose of giving effect to the will of the judge; always for the purpose of giving effect ... to the will of the law."

Step Four: Reject Court-Made Or Evolutionary Law

Justice Kennedy and his four majority colleagues are at odds with Moses, Blackstone and Marshall. They believe that law "evolve[s] over time," and that it is the role of the judge to bring "new insights" to bear on the "changed understandings of marriage [which] are characteristic of a Nation where new dimensions of freedom; become apparent to new generations." As Chief Justice Roberts wrote in dissent, Kennedy and his co-signers exalt "the role of the judiciary in delivering social change":

> Those who founded this country would not recognize the majority's conception of the judicial role. They after all risked their lives and fortunes for the precious right to govern themselves. They would never have imagined yielding that right on a question of social policy to unaccountable and unelected judges.

This claim of power, Justice Scalia observed in his dissent, is "a naked judicial claim to legislative — indeed, super-legislative — power."

This naked claim to power prompted Chief Justice Roberts to ask the question: "Just who do we think we are?" According to Justice Kennedy, it is the Court's job to keep the 18th century Constitution up-to-date:

> The generations that wrote and ratified the Bill of Rights and the Fourteenth

> Amendment did not presume to know the extent of freedom in all of its dimensions, and so they entrusted to future generations a charter protecting the right of all persons to enjoy liberty as we learn its meaning. When new insight reveals discord between the Constitution's central protections and a received legal structure, a claim to liberty must be addressed.

Addressed by whom? And how? Surely not by judges and the judicial process. As Justice Scalia clearly noted in his dissent, there is a clear process for "a claim of liberty" to be addressed by future generations: amendments. Indeed, both the Bill of Rights and the Fourteenth Amendment addressed new claims of liberty, but neither were added to the Constitution by the Supreme Court. To the contrary, both changes came through one of the two processes provided for constitutional changes under Article V of the Constitution:

> Congress, whenever two thirds of both Houses shall deem it necessary, shall propose amendments to this Constitution, or, on application of the legislatures of two thirds of the several States, shall call a convention for proposing amendments, which, in either case, shall be valid to all intents and purposes, as part of this Constitution, when ratified by the legislatures of three fourths of the several States, or by conventions of three-fourths thereof, as the one or the other mode of ratification may be proposed by Congress....

By its plain language, Article V prescribes that the task of changing the Constitution to meet changing times is vested completely in Congress and in the 50 state legislatures, not the Supreme Court and such other courts as Congress may from time to time provide under Article III of the Constitution.[13] Further, such changes are not to come about by a simple majority vote. Rather, amendments to the Constitution cannot even be considered without a two-thirds vote in either Congress or fifty state legislatures. Even then, such amendments cannot be made to the constitution without a favorable vote of three-fourths of the state legislatures or of the delegates to a convention called by three-fourth of the States.

Throwing this prescribed constitutional caution to the wind, the same-sex marriage majority justices claim for themselves the unfettered right to determine whether a "new" constitutional claim should be decided by them via the ordinary judicial process of Article III (such as the right to same-sex marriage), or relegated to Congress and the fifty state legislatures and the extraordinary amendment process of Article V (such as the right of physician-assisted suicide). As to which process applies to which right, it depends upon whether the group seeking constitutional protection is sufficiently "disparaged," "demeaned," or "stigmatized," to earn the empathy of the Court.

In short, Justice Kennedy believes that it is up to the Court — not Congress or the fifty state legislatures — to determine whether it is "necessary" to amend the Constitution. According to Article

V of the Constitution, however, it is the People, acting through their elected representatives in Congress and in the legislatures of the fifty states, who have this authority. No wonder that Justice Scalia pronounced the majority's christening of same-sex marriage a "judicial Putsch," a seizure of the sovereignty of the People, deriving unjust powers without their consent.

Step Five: Call For Interposition By The States

Next, we can call on state leaders to declare *Obergefell* unconstitutional and refuse to enforce any unconstitutional aspects of the opinion. In our modern era, the idea of anything but submitting entirely to a Supreme Court opinion is looked upon suspiciously. But, as noted earlier— every citizen has a sworn duty to defend the Constitution. That is our highest oath of allegiance. The governors and legislators of the states do not swear allegiance to a president or a federal government or a court ruling. We need to hold them accountable to their higher allegiance. And there is a mechanism for state officials to resist an unconstitutional ruling. It's called "interposition."

Writing in *Federalist No. 78,* Alexander Hamilton reassured his fellow patriots that they need not fear the Constitution's creation of an independent judicial branch because, "from the nature of its functions," the judiciary "will always be the least dangerous to the political rights of the constitution; because it will be in a least capacity to annoy or injure them." Backing up his prophecy, Hamilton contrasted the powers of each of the three branches, noting that the President "holds the sword of the community," Congress the "purse," leaving the courts with "neither force nor will, but merely judgment."

As it has turned out, however, Hamilton underestimated the power of "reasoned judgment" cloaked in judicial robes, and overestimated the check upon a tyrannical judiciary by the President and Congress, as well as by the Governors and legislatures of the several States. To be sure, Hamilton correctly pointed out, federal judges are totally dependent upon the President, as confirmed by the fact that the Supreme Court's order desegregating the schools did not prove fully effective until President Eisenhower federalized the National Guard in Arkansas forcing the admission of African American children to Little Rock High School. But Hamilton did not foresee the adverse impact that this event would have on today's Governors who are immediately branded as an outlaw should they even hint that they would, like Orval Faubus and George Wallace, stand in the way of the enforcement of a Supreme Court order, no matter how unlawful.

So it came as no surprise that on the very day that the Supreme Court handed down its same-sex marriage order, Governors of almost every State, proclaimed — without even reading the opinion or awaiting the 25-day waiting period before the order went into effect — that marriage licenses would be issued to same-sex couples.

Such action is being justified as required by "the rule of law." But it is not. As the chief executive officer of the state, every Governor is duty bound by oath to take care that the law is faithfully executed. Thus, he has a constitutional responsibility **before** deciding to enforce a court order — even an order of the United States Supreme Court — to determine if the Court order is lawful. This power to interpose between the people and the Court is what is known as the authority of the lower civil magistrate. While the ultimate authority to enforce an order of the United States Supreme Court is vested in the President, that does not excuse a Governor, as a lower civil magistrate, from his sworn duty to decide whether a Supreme Court order blocking the enforcement of a state law — like the laws defining marriage to exclude same-sex couples — is lawful under the United States Constitution. To automatically assume, as the nation's Governors appear to have done, that they must defer to the President's ultimate authority to decide whether a Supreme Court order is lawful, is contrary to their duty as lower civil magistrates.

The doctrine of the lesser magistrate was well-established at the time of the nation's founding.[14] Indeed, the nation's charter — the Declaration of Independence — is predicated upon the right of the people's elected representatives meeting in Congress assembled to interpose themselves between King George III and the English Parliament and the American people to protect the people's right to govern themselves according to the law of nature and of nature's

God. After all, under Romans 13:4, whoever wields civil power does so as a servant of God, and is duty bound by God to rule according to the law, not according to a superior civil officer who is acting in violation of the law.

Applying this doctrine to the *Obergefell* order, the four dissenting justices provided ample evidence and argument that the order was unconstitutional, justifying State interposition. The fact that the Court was deeply divided at 5-4 adds credence to a gubernatorial decision to order state or local civil officers not to issue marriage licenses to same-sex couples. By taking such action, the Governor would protect the state and local government officials from having to make that decision individually. And, by taking such action, the Governors would place the issue of enforcement squarely into the President's lap where it belongs, the President being the nation's chief executive officer with the duty of taking care that the law is faithfully executed.

Step Six: Congressional Action

In Federalist No. 58, James Madison wrote that the "power of the purse may, in fact, be regarded as the most complete and effectual weapon with which any constitution can arm the immediate representatives of the people, for redress of every grievance, and for carrying into effect every just and salutary measure." In Federalist 78, Alexander Hamilton reminds us that, Congress' power of the purse is a check and balance even on the federal courts.

In the immediate aftermath of the Supreme Court's decision in *Roe v. Wade*, striking down the fifty states' laws prohibiting abortion, Congress stepped into action to protect doctors, hospitals and others from being required to violate their consciences with respect to their religious and moral objections to the killing of the unborn.[15] Additionally, through passage of the Hyde Amendment, there has existed a ban upon taxpayer funding of abortions. At stake, then, was the concern that with the judicial declaration of a constitutional right to an abortion, there would follow government mandates forcing people to support abortion.

As noted above, that same threat has already materialized regarding the Court's decision sanctioning same-sex marriage. One means available to protect the people from being forced to act against one's conscientious objection to the newly minted right to same-sex marriage, and the anti-discrimination cases that go with it, is to attach to appropriation bills (i) bans against the use of federal funds to support so-called "alternative sex lifestyles," and (ii) conditions placed upon recipients of federal funds requiring schools and other organizations to abandon their religious and moral objections to same-sex relationships.

Already, the Senate has held hearings on "judicial activism" to the end of limiting the jurisdiction of federal courts, as provided for in Article III, Section 2 of the Constitution. While efforts to curb jurisdictions have not been very successful in the past, the holding of hearings and airing of grievances against a runaway judicial system can have a sobering effect. Threats of impeachment can also have a similar impact, but it is highly unlikely that Congress, even though there is a Republican majority in both houses, would act. Nonetheless calls for impeachment may very well have an impact on the public, increasing their awareness of the need for changes in both the personnel and practices on the court. Therefore, it is important to note that after the Supreme Court's controversial rulings on same-sex marriage and ObamaCare in June 2015, a Pew Research poll indicated that "unfavorable opinions of the Supreme Court have reached a 30-year high."

Step Seven: Elect A Constitutional President

The President of the United States is the nation's chief constitutional officer. According to the presidential oath printed in Article II of the Constitution, the President, and he alone, is sworn to "preserve, protect, and defend" the Constitution of the United States. All other officers — state and federal, executive, legislative, and judicial — are sworn only to "support" the Constitution. Why the difference? The President holds the sword, the power of enforcement. And because he does, he poses the greatest danger to the Constitution, for he can do the most damage to our constitutional order, and yet, by honoring the Constitution, he inspires his countrymen by not overusing the executive powers exclusively vested in him.

The current President has not been shy to use the power of his office to accomplish his transformative goals to change America. At every point, he has stretched his powers to the cutting edge, even after he previously announced that the Constitution did not allow him to do what he then did. As for same-sex marriage, the President first told the American people that he opposed it. Yet, the President and his Department of Justice did everything they could to undermine the Defense of Marriage Act passed into law by wide margins during the Clinton administration. Not surprisingly, the President enthusiastically welcomed the Supreme Court's same-sex marriage ruling, sending the clear signal to the nation's Governors that those States that had not voluntarily changed their rules governing marriage would receive no help from the White House. Running at top speed, the President is implementing the Court's same-sex marriage edict throughout the structure of the federal government.

In that same spirit, the Equal Employment Opportunity Commission has changed its view that the federal anti-discrimination laws do not protect persons from being discriminated on account of sexual orientation. Bypassing Congress, the EEOC now claims that sex discrimination is broad enough to encompass sexual orientation. After all, if the President can bypass Congress on immigration, what is there to stop the EEOC from unilaterally acting against discrimination on the basis of sexual orientation now that the Supreme Court has decreed that sexual orientation is an immutable characteristic, like race or sex.

Step Eight: Amend The Court Or The Constitution

At the heart of judicial power is the claim that law is fixed as to time, uniform as to the person, and universal as to place. If a rule never changes, and if it applies equally without respect of persons, and does not change from place to place, such a rule commands our respect, deserving one's obedience. But if a rule is given to change, and honors the rich over the poor, and applies in one place, but not in another, the opposite is true. Such a rule deserves our disrespect.

Now that the Supreme Court has ruled that there is a constitutional right for same-sex couples to marry, any effort to change that ruling, which was made by the narrowest of margins, will be very difficult. A judicial decision must have at least the appearance of impartiality, or it will look like a political, not like a legal, decision. If a member of the *Obergefell* majority should resign from the Court or die, and a new justice be appointed to the court, a 5 to 4 vote going the other way would open the court to the criticism that its decisions are political, not legal, and even worse, political behind closed doors. And even worse than that, a decision made by unelected judges who hold their office for life. Hence, the court would be subject not just to the criticism that their decision was wrong, but that it was illegitimate — one that should have been made by the people's representatives — and therefore, unworthy of respect.

To be sure, the Supreme Court has changed its mind, overruling prior cases, but only where there is the strongest of grounds, and only when enough time has passed that the people forget. But the more controversial the opinion, and the more widespread its dissemination, the more time needs to transpire for the public memory to fade away. For example, few people know that for the Supreme Court to establish the right of a same-sex couple to marry in *Obergefell*, it was required to overrule an obscure case decided in 1972, 43 years before. Even then, that case was a "one-line summary decision," unknown to the public and unknown to the bar, except when it was dredged up to combat efforts in lower federal courts to establish a same-sex marriage claim because of a governing Supreme Court precedent. Still, the Court felt it necessary to bury the 1972 case under a barrage of "other more instructive precedents" before overruling it.

With such institutional barriers available to the Court to protect its mirage of near infallibility, it would come as no surprise to learn that opponents of a controversial Supreme Court ruling, such as its abortion ruling in 1973, choose to amend the Constitution, even though it is not the Constitution that needs amending, but the Court. As noted above, however, the amendment process has been successful only when there are substantial majorities in favor, a very unlikely prospect in any effort to overrule a sharply divided court.

Step Nine: Resistance To Same-Sex Bigotry

Justice Kennedy went out of his way to assure those who oppose same sex marriage that the Court's ruling does not "disparage" their religious or philosophical views. Rather, he contended, the Court's ruling only condemns those views when they "becom[e] enacted law and public policy, the necessary consequence [of which] is to put the imprimitur of the State itself on an exclusion that soon demeans or stigmatizes those whose own liberty is then denied." To remove this stigma, the Court decreed that "[u]nder the Constitution, same-sex couples [are] entitled] to the same treatment as opposite-sex couples, and it would disparage their choices and diminish their personhood to deny them this right."

Not surprisingly, the LGBT community has seized on this constitutional guarantee of "equality" to employ the full force of the law to stop businesses from discriminating against same-sex couples on the ground that such decisions demean and disparage them. Christian-owned businesses will face the most daunting gauntlet in the wake of *Obergefell*. The Equal Employment Opportunity Commission has already issued a ruing expanding its protections for sexual orientation to the same level as race or sex. There is no "Christian/religious" barrier any more at the EEOC. Christian business owners should expect to be targeted for harassment suits like never before. Each time will present an opportunity for Christians to stand, in humility, on their religious liberties and the

Constitution. The cost may be high. One bakery owner is being forced to pay more than $100,000 in punitive fees *directly to a lesbian couple* simply because they refused to bake a cake for a lesbian wedding. Even worse, overwhelming death threats and a targeted hate campaign forced them to close their business.

In his dissent, Justice Samuel Alito predicted tougher times ahead for those who do not hold to the Court's mandated same-sex edict:

> I assume that those who cling to old beliefs will be able to whisper their thoughts in the recesses of their homes, but if they repeat those views in public, they will risk being labeled as bigots and treated as such by governments, employers and schools.

According to Justice Kennedy, however, "the First Amendment ensures that religious organizations and persons are given **proper protection** as they seek to teach the principles that are so fulfilling and **central** to their **lives and faiths**, and to their own deep aspirations to continue the family structure they have so long revered." If the First Amendment only protects the teaching of "religious doctrine," without also putting such teaching of "the principles ...central to their lives and faiths" into practice, the First Amendment will prove to be no shield to laws that prohibit as discriminatory those actions that are commanded by that faith. "Ominously," Chief Justice Roberts wrote in his dissent, "[the freedom to 'exercise' religion] is not a word the majority uses."

In order to put into practice what they preach, then, churches, Christian businesses and individual believers – and others who are like minded – must put into practice what they truly believe. With the examples of Peter and John before us, we too must stand before the judicial tribunals of our day and boldly proclaim: "We must obey God rather than men."

Step Ten (Most Important): Don't Give Up!

In Isaiah 28, the prophet speaks of an Israel, not much different from the United States in which we live. The prophet observes that the nation, full of pride, has turned it back on God, having made a covenant with death and an agreement with hell, covering both up with a refuge of lies. But, as was true in Israel then, so it is true in America today, God laid a cornerstone of hope and faith in which He called the people to believe. That cornerstone is Jesus Christ, the Lord of Lords and King of Kings. Through that cornerstone God strips away the lies, exposing the nation's covenant with death and agreement with hell, reminding the two nations that a nation that attempts to live contrary to God's law is like a man who attempts to sleep in a bed that is too short and under a cover that is too narrow. But God does not leave the nation there. Rather, the prophet reminds us of the time when King David broke through to defeat the Philistines, and God gave the Amorites over to Joshua, as the sun stood still.

As was true in Israel, so it is true in America. God is stripping away the lies of Planned Parenthood, ending its tyranny of euphemisms, with true accounts of their gruesome and bloody practices, videoed by the Center for Medical Progress for the whole world to see abortion for what it really is — a covenant with death. And already, the truth is bubbling up out of the depths of hell for the people to see what same-sex marriage is really about, as the new totalitarians move from business to business, from school to school, from church to church to force people to "tolerate" their filthy sex habits in broad day light for all to see — an agreement with hell.

It is not time to retreat, but to stand. For God has laid the cornerstone and we that believe shall not run away. Truth and life will prevail!

Appendix

No Basis In The Constitution

Chief Justice John G Roberts

CHIEF JUSTICE ROBERTS, with whom JUSTICE SCALIA and JUSTICE THOMAS join, dissenting.

Petitioners make strong arguments rooted in social policy and considerations of fairness. They contend that same-sex couples should be allowed to affirm their love and commitment through marriage, just like opposite-sex couples. That position has undeniable appeal; over the past six years, voters and legislators in eleven States and the District of Columbia have revised their laws to allow marriage between two people of the same sex.

But this Court is not a legislature. Whether same-sex marriage is a good idea should be of no concern to us. Under the Constitution, judges have power to say what the law is, not what it should be. The people who ratified the Constitution authorized courts to exercise "neither force nor will but merely judgment." *The Federalist* No. 78, p. 465 (C. Rossiter ed. 1961) (A. Hamilton) (capitalization altered).

Although the policy arguments for extending marriage to same-sex couples may be compelling, the legal arguments for requiring such an extension are not. The fundamental right to marry does not include a right to make a State change its definition of marriage. And a State's decision to maintain the meaning of marriage that has persisted in every culture throughout human history can hardly be called irrational. In short, our Constitution does not enact any one theory of marriage. The people of a State are free to expand marriage to include same-sex couples, or to retain the historic definition.

Today, however, the Court takes the extraordinary step of ordering every State to license and recognize same-sex marriage. Many people will rejoice at this decision, and I begrudge none their celebration. But for those who believe in a government of laws, not of men, the majority's approach is deeply disheartening. Supporters of same-sex marriage have achieved considerable success persuading their fellow citizens—through the democratic process—to adopt their view. That ends today. Five lawyers have closed the debate and enacted their own vision of marriage as a matter of constitutional law. Stealing this issue from the people will for many cast a cloud over same-sex marriage, making a dramatic social change that much more difficult to accept.

The majority's decision is an act of will, not legal judgment. The right it announces has no basis in the Constitution or this Court's precedent. The majority expressly disclaims judicial "caution" and omits even a pretense of humility, openly relying on its desire to remake society according to its own "new insight" into the "nature of injustice." *Ante*, at 11, 23. As a result, the Court invalidates the marriage laws of more than half the States and orders the transformation of a social institution that has formed the basis of human society for millennia, for the Kalahari Bushmen and the Han Chinese, the Carthaginians and the Aztecs. Just who do we think we are?

It can be tempting for judges to confuse our own preferences with the requirements of the law. But as this Court has been reminded throughout our history, the Constitution "is made for people of fundamentally differing views." *Lochner v. New York*, 198 U.S. 45, 76 (1905) (Holmes, J., dissenting). Accordingly, "courts are not concerned with the wisdom or policy of legislation." Id., at 69 (Harlan, J., dissenting). The majority today neglects that restrained conception of the judicial role. It seizes for itself a question the Constitution leaves to the people, at a time when the people are engaged in a vibrant debate on that question. And it answers that question based not on neutral principles of constitutional law, but on its own "understanding of what freedom is and must become." Ante, at 19. I have no choice but to dissent.

Understand well what this dissent is about: It is not about whether, in my judgment, the institution of marriage should be changed to include same-sex couples. It is instead about whether, in our democratic republic, that decision should rest with the people acting through their elected representatives, or with five lawyers who happen to hold commissions authorizing them to resolve legal disputes according to law. The Constitution leaves no doubt about the answer.

I

Petitioners and their *amici* base their arguments on the" right to marry" and the imperative of "marriage equality." There is no serious dispute that, under our precedents, the Constitution protects a right to marry and requires States to apply their marriage laws equally. The real question in these cases is what constitutes "marriage," or—more precisely—who decides what constitutes "marriage"? The majority largely ignores these questions, relegating ages of human experience with marriage to a paragraph or two. Even if history and precedent are not "the end" of these cases, ante, at 4, I would not "sweep away what has so long been settled" without showing greater respect for all that preceded us. *Town of Greece v. Galloway,* 572 U.S. ___, ___ (2014) (slip op., at 8).

A

As the majority acknowledges, marriage "has existed for millennia and across civilizations." *Ante*, at 3. For all those millennia, across all those civilizations, "marriage" referred to only one relationship: the union of a man and a woman. See *ante*, at 4; Tr. of Oral Arg. on Question 1, p. 12 (petitioners conceding that they are not aware of any society that permitted same-sex marriage before 2001). As the Court explained two Terms ago, "until recent years, ... marriage between a man and a woman no doubt had been thought of by most people as essential to the very definition of that term and to its role and function throughout the history of civilization." *United States v. Windsor*, 570 U.S. ___, ___ (2013) (slip op., at 13).

This universal definition of marriage as the union of a man and a woman is no historical coincidence. Marriage did not come about as a result of a political movement, discovery, disease, war, religious doctrine, or any other moving force of world history—and certainly not as a result of a prehistoric decision to exclude gays and lesbians. It arose in the nature of things to meet a vital need: ensuring that children are conceived by a mother and father committed to raising them in the stable conditions of a lifelong relationship. See G. Quale, *A History of Marriage Systems 2* (1988); cf. M. Cicero, *De Officiis* 57 (W. Miller transl. 1913) ("For since the reproductive instinct is by nature's gift the common possession of all living creatures, the first bond of union is that between husband and wife; the next, that between parents and children; then we find one home, with everything in common.").

The premises supporting this concept of marriage are so fundamental that they rarely require articulation. The human race must procreate to survive. Procreation occurs through sexual relations between a man and a woman. When sexual relations result in the conception of a child, that child's prospects are generally better if the mother and father stay together rather than going their separate ways. Therefore, for the good of children and society, sexual relations that can lead to procreation should occur only between a man and a woman committed to a lasting bond.

Society has recognized that bond as marriage. And by bestowing a respected status and material benefits on married couples, society encourages men and women to conduct sexual relations within marriage rather than without. As one prominent scholar put it, "Marriage is a socially arranged solution for the problem of getting people to stay together and care for children that the mere desire for children, and the sex that makes children possible, does not solve." J. Q. Wilson, *The Marriage Problem* 41 (2002).

This singular understanding of marriage has prevailed in the United States throughout our history. The majority accepts that at "the time of the Nation's founding [marriage] was understood to be a voluntary contract between a man and a woman." Ante, at 6. Early Americans drew heavily on legal scholars like William Blackstone, who regarded marriage between "husband and wife" as one of the "great relations in private life," and philosophers like John Locke, who described marriage as "a voluntary compact between man and woman" centered on "its chief end, procreation" and the "nourishment and support" of children. 1 *W. Blackstone, Commentaries* *410; J. Locke, *Second Treatise of Civil Government* §§78–79, p. 39 (J. Gough ed. 1947). To those who drafted and ratified the Constitution, this conception of marriage and family "was a given: its structure, its stability, roles, and values accepted by all." Forte, *The Framers' Idea of Marriag*e and Family, in *The Meaning of Marriage* 100, 102 (R. George & J. Elshtain eds. 2006).

The Constitution itself says nothing about marriage, and the Framers thereby entrusted the States with "[t]he whole subject of the domestic relations of husband and wife." *Windsor,* 570 U.S., at ___ (slip op., at 17) (quoting *In re Burrus,* 136 U.S. 586, 593–594 (1890)). There is no dispute that every State at the founding—and every State throughout our history until a dozen years ago—defined marriage in the traditional, biologically rooted way. The four States in these cases are typical. Their laws, before and after statehood, have treated marriage as the union of a man and a woman. See *DeBoer v. Snyder,* 772 F. 3d 388, 396–399 (CA6 2014). Even when state laws did not specify this definition expressly, no one doubted what they meant. See *Jones v. Hallahan,* 501 S. W. 2d 588, 589 (Ky. App. 1973). The meaning of "marriage" went without saying.

Of course, many did say it. In his first American dictionary, Noah Webster defined marriage as "the legal union of a man and woman for life," which served the purposes of "preventing the promiscuous intercourse of the sexes, ... promoting domestic felicity, and ... securing the maintenance and education of children." 1 *An American Dictionary of the English Language* (1828). An influential 19th-century treatise defined marriage as "a civil status, existing in one man and one woman legally united for life for those civil and social purposes which are based in the distinction of sex." J. Bishop, *Commentaries on the Law of Marriage and Divorce* 25 (1852). The first edition of *Black's Law Dictionary* defined marriage as "the civil status of one man and one woman united in law for life." *Black's Law Dictionary* 756 (1891) (emphasis deleted). The dictionary maintained essentially that same definition for the next century.

This Court's precedents have repeatedly described marriage in ways that are consistent only with its traditional meaning. Early cases on the subject referred to marriage as "the union for life of one man and one woman," *Murphy* v. *Ramsey*, 114 U.S. 15, 45 (1885), which forms "the foundation of the family and of society, without which there would be neither civilization nor progress," *Maynard* v. *Hill*, 125 U.S. 190, 211 (1888). We later described marriage as "fundamental to our very existence and survival," an understanding that necessarily implies a procreative component. *Loving* v. *Virginia*, 388 U.S. 1, 12 (1967); see *Skinner* v. *Oklahoma* ex rel. Williamson, 316 U.S. 535, 541 (1942). More recent cases have directly connected the right to marry with the "right to procreate." *Zablocki* v. *Redhail*, 434 U.S. 374, 386 (1978).

As the majority notes, some aspects of marriage have changed over time. Arranged marriages have largely given way to pairings based on romantic love. States have replaced coverture, the doctrine by which a married man and woman became a single legal entity, with laws that respect each participant's separate status. Racial restrictions on marriage, which "arose as an incident to slavery" to promote "White Supremacy," were repealed by many States and ultimately struck down by this Court. *Loving*, 388 U.S., at 6–7.

The majority observes that these developments "were not mere superficial changes" in marriage, but rather "worked deep transformations in its structure." *Ante*, at 6–7. They did not, however, work any transformation in the core structure of marriage as the union between a man and a woman. If you had asked a person on the street how marriage was defined, no one would ever have said, "Marriage is the union of a man and a woman, where the woman is subject to coverture." The majority may be right that the "history of marriage is one of both continuity and change," but the core meaning of marriage has endured. *Ante*, at 6.

B

Shortly after this Court struck down racial restrictions on marriage in Loving, a gay couple in Minnesota sought a marriage license. They argued that the Constitution required States to allow marriage between people of the same sex for the same reasons that it requires States to allow marriage between people of different races. The Minnesota Supreme Court rejected their analogy to Loving, and this Court summarily dismissed an appeal. *Baker* v. *Nelson*, 409 U.S. 810 (1972).

In the decades after *Baker*, greater numbers of gays and lesbians began living openly, and many expressed a desire to have their relationships recognized as marriages. Over time, more people came to see marriage in a way that could be extended to such couples. Until recently, this new view of marriage remained a minority position.

After the Massachusetts Supreme Judicial Court in 2003 interpreted its State Constitution to require recognition of same-sex marriage, many States—including the four at issue here—enacted constitutional amendments formally adopting the longstanding definition of marriage.

Over the last few years, public opinion on marriage has shifted rapidly. In 2009, the legislatures of Vermont, New Hampshire, and the District of Columbia became the first in the Nation to enact laws that revised the definition of marriage to include same-sex couples, while also providing accommodations for religious believers. In 2011, the New York Legislature enacted a similar law. In 2012, voters in Maine did the same, reversing the result of a referendum just three years earlier in which they had upheld the traditional definition of marriage.

In all, voters and legislators in eleven States and the District of Columbia have changed their definitions of marriage to include same-sex couples. The highest courts of five States have decreed that same result under their own Constitutions. The remainder of the States retain the traditional definition of marriage.

Petitioners brought lawsuits contending that the *Due Process* and *Equal Protection* Clauses of the Fourteenth Amendment compel their States to license and recognize marriages between same-sex couples. In a carefully reasoned decision, the Court of Appeals acknowledged the democratic "momentum" in favor of "expand[ing] the definition of marriage to include gay couples," but concluded that petitioners had not made "the case for constitutionalizing the definition of marriage and for removing the issue from the place it has been since the founding: in the hands of state voters." 772 F. 3d, at 396, 403. That decision interpreted the Constitution correctly, and I would affirm.

II

Petitioners first contend that the marriage laws of their States violate the Due Process Clause. The Solicitor General of the United States, appearing in support of petitioners, expressly disowned that position before this Court. See *Tr. of Oral Arg.* on Question 1, at 38–39. The majority nevertheless resolves these cases for petitioners based almost entirely on the *Due Process Clause*.

The majority purports to identify four "principles and traditions" in this Court's due process precedents that support a fundamental right for same-sex couples to marry. *Ante*, at 12. In reality, however, the majority's approach has no basis in principle or tradition, except for the unprincipled tradition of judicial policymaking that characterized discredited decisions such as *Lochner v. New York*, 198 U.S. 45. Stripped of its shiny rhetorical gloss, the majority's argument is that the *Due Process Clause* gives same-sex couples a fundamental right to marry because it will be good for them and for society. If I were a legislator, I would certainly consider that view as a matter of social policy. But as a judge, I find the majority's position indefensible as a matter of constitutional law.

A

Petitioners' "fundamental right" claim falls into the most sensitive category of constitutional adjudication. Petitioners do not contend that their States' marriage laws violate an enumerated constitutional right, such as the freedom of speech protected by the First Amendment. There is, after all, no "Companionship and Understanding" or "Nobility and Dignity" Clause in the Constitution. See ante, at 3, 14. They argue instead that the laws violate a right implied by the Fourteenth Amendment's requirement that "liberty" may not be deprived without "due process of law."

This Court has interpreted the Due Process Clause to include a "substantive" component that protects certain liberty interests against state deprivation "no matter what process is provided." *Reno v. Flores*, 507 U.S. 292, 302 (1993). The theory is that some liberties are "so rooted in the traditions and conscience of our people as to be ranked as fundamental," and therefore cannot be deprived without compelling justification. *Snyder v. Massachusetts*, allowing unelected federal judges to select which unenumerated rights rank as "fundamental"—and to strike down state laws on the basis of that determination—raises obvious concerns about the judicial role. Our precedents have accordingly insisted that judges "exercise the utmost care" in identifying implied fundamental rights, "lest the liberty protected by the Due Process Clause be subtly transformed into the policy preferences of the Members of this Court." *Washington v. Glucksberg*, 521 U.S. 702,

720 (1997) (internal quotation marks omitted); see Kennedy, Unenumerated Rights and the Dictates of Judicial Restraint 13 (1986) (Address at Stanford) ("One can conclude that certain essential, or fundamental, rights should exist in any just society. It does not follow that each of those essential rights is one that we as judges can enforce under the written Constitution. The Due Process Clause is not a guarantee of every right that should inhere in an ideal system.").

The need for restraint in administering the strong medicine of substantive due process is a lesson this Court has learned the hard way. The Court first applied substantive due process to strike down a statute in *Dred Scott v. Sandford*, 19 How. 393 (1857). There the Court invalidated the Missouri Compromise on the ground that legislation restricting the institution of slavery violated the implied rights of slaveholders. The Court relied on its own conception of liberty and property in doing so. It asserted that "an act of Congress which deprives a citizen of the United States of his liberty or property, merely because he came himself or brought his property into a particular territory of the United States ... could hardly be dignified with the name of due process of law." Id., at 450. In a dissent that has outlasted the majority opinion, Justice Curtis explained that when the "fixed rules which govern the interpretation of laws [are] abandoned, and the theoretical opinions of individuals are allowed to control" the Constitution's meaning, "we have no longer a Constitution; we are under the government of individual men, who for the time being have power to declare what the Constitution is, according to their own views of what it ought to mean." Id., at 621.

Dred Scott's holding was overruled on the battlefields of the Civil War and by constitutional amendment after Appomattox, but its approach to the Due Process Clause reappeared. In a series of early 20th-century cases, most prominently *Lochner* v. *New York,* this Court invalidated state statutes that presented meddlesome interferences with the rights of the individual," and "undue interference with liberty of person and freedom of contract." 198 U.S., at 60, 61. In *Lochner* itself, the Court struck down a New York law setting maximum hours for bakery employees, because there was "in our judgment, no reasonable foundation for holding this to be necessary or appropriate as a health law." Id., at 58.

The dissenting Justices in *Lochner* explained that the New York law could be viewed as a reasonable response to legislative concern about the health of bakery employees, an issue on which there was at least "room for debate and for an honest difference of opinion." Id., at 72 (opinion of Harlan, J.). The majority's contrary conclusion required adopting as constitutional law "an economic theory which a large part of the country does not entertain." Id., at 75 (opinion of Holmes, J.). As Justice Holmes memorably put it, "The Fourteenth Amendment does not enact Mr. Herbert Spencer's Social Statics," a leading work on the philosophy of Social Darwinism. Ibid. The Constitution "is not intended to embody a particular economic theory.... It is made for people of fundamentally differing views, and the accident of our finding certain opinions natural and familiar or novel and even shocking ought not to conclude our judgment upon the question whether statutes embodying them conflict with the Constitution." Id., at 75–76.

In the decades after *Lochner*, the Court struck down nearly 200 laws as violations of individual liberty, often over strong dissents contending that "[t]he criterion of constitutionality is not whether we believe the law to before the public good." *Adkins v. Children's Hospital of D. C.*, 261 U.S. 525, 570 (1923) (opinion of Holmes, J.). By empowering judges to elevate their own policy judgments to the status of constitutionally protected "liberty," the *Lochner* line of cases left "no alternative to regarding the court as a ... legislative chamber." L. Hand, The Bill of Rights 42 (1958).

Eventually, the Court recognized its error and vowed not to repeat it. "The doctrine that ... due process authorizes courts to hold laws unconstitutional when they believe the legislature has acted unwisely," we later explained, "has long since been discarded. We have returned to the original constitutional proposition that courts do not substitute their social and economic beliefs for the judgment of legislative bodies, who are elected to pass laws." *Ferguson v. Skrupa*, 372 U.S. 726, 730 (1963); see *Day-Brite Lighting, Inc. v. Missouri*, 342 U.S. 421, 423 (1952) ("we do not sit as a super-legislature to weigh the wisdom of legislation"). Thus, it has become an accepted rule that the Court will not hold laws unconstitutional simply because we find them "unwise, improvident, or out of harmony with a particular school of thought." *Williamson v. Lee Optical of Okla., Inc.*, 348 U.S. 483, 488 (1955).

Rejecting *Lochner* does not require disavowing the doctrine of implied fundamental rights, and this Court has not done so. But to avoid repeating *Lochner*'s error of converting personal preferences into constitutional mandates, our modern substantive due process cases have stressed the need for "judicial self-restraint." *Collins v. Harker Heights*, 503 U.S. 115, 125 (1992). Our precedents have required that implied fundamental rights be "objectively, deeply rooted in this Nation's history and tradition," and "implicit in the concept of ordered liberty, such that neither liberty nor justice would exist if they were sacrificed." *Glucksberg*, 521 U.S., at 720–721 (internal quotation marks omitted).

Although the Court articulated the importance of history and tradition to the fundamental rights inquiry most precisely in *Glucksberg*, many other cases both before and after have adopted the same approach. See, e.g., *District Attorney's Office for Third Judicial Dist.* v. *Osborne*, 557 U.S. 52, 72 (2009); *Flores*, 507 U.S., at 303; *United States* v. *Salerno*, 481 U.S. 739, 751 (1987); *Moore* v. *East Cleveland*, 431 U.S. 494, 503 (1977) (plurality opinion); see also id., at 544 (White, J., dissenting) ("The Judiciary, including this Court, is the most vulnerable and comes nearest to illegitimacy when it deals with judge-made constitutional law having little or no cognizable roots in the language or even the design of the

Constitution."); *Troxel* v. *Granville*, 530 U.S. 57, 96–101 (2000) (KENNEDY, J., dissenting) (consulting "'[o]ur Nation's history, legal traditions, and practices'" and concluding that "[w]e owe it to the Nation's domestic relations legal structure ... to proceed with caution" (quoting *Glucksberg*, 521 U.S., at 721)).

Proper reliance on history and tradition of course requires looking beyond the individual law being challenged, so that every restriction on liberty does not supply its own constitutional justification. The Court is right about that. *Ante*, at 18. But given the few "guideposts for responsible decision making in this unchartered area," *Collins*, 503 U.S., at 125, "an approach grounded in history imposes limits on the judiciary that are more meaningful than any based on [an] abstract formula," *Moore*, 431 U.S., at 504, n. 12 (plurality opinion). Expanding a right suddenly and dramatically is likely to require tearing it up from its roots. Even a sincere profession of "discipline" in identifying fundamental rights, *ante*, at 10–11, does not provide a meaningful constraint on a judge, for "what he is really likely to be 'discovering,' whether or not he is fully aware of it, are his own values," J. Ely, Democracy and Distrust44 (1980). The only way to ensure restraint in this delicate enterprise is "continual insistence upon respect for the teachings of history, solid recognition of the basic values that underlie our society, and wise appreciation of the great roles [of] the doctrines of federalism and separation of powers." *Griswold v. Connecticut*, 381 U.S. 479, 501 (1965) (Harlan, J., concurring in judgment).

B

The majority acknowledges none of this doctrinal background, and it is easy to see why: Its aggressive application of substantive due process breaks sharply with decades of precedent and returns the Court to the unprincipled approach of *Lochner*.

1

The majority's driving themes are that marriage is desirable and petitioners desire it. The opinion describes the "transcendent importance" of marriage and repeatedly insists that petitioners do not seek to "demean," "devalue,""denigrate," or "disrespect" the institution. Ante, at 3, 4, 6, 28. Nobody disputes those points. Indeed, the compelling personal accounts of petitioners and others like them are likely a primary reason why many Americans have changed their minds about whether same-sex couples should be allowed to marry. As a matter of constitutional law, however, the sincerity of petitioners' wishes is not relevant.

When the majority turns to the law, it relies primarily on precedents discussing the fundamental "right to marry." *Turner v. Safley*, 482 U.S. 78, 95 (1987); *Zablocki*, 434 U.S., at 383; see *Loving*, 388 U.S., at 12. These cases do not hold, of course, that anyone who wants to get married has a constitutional right to do so. They instead require a State to justify barriers to marriage as that institution has always been understood. In Loving, the Court held that racial restrictions on the right to marry lacked a compelling justification. In *Zablocki*, restrictions based on child support debts did not suffice. In *Turner*, restrictions based on status as a prisoner were deemed impermissible.

None of the laws at issue in those cases purported to change the core definition of marriage as the union of a man and a woman. The laws challenged in *Zablocki* and *Turner* did not define marriage as "the union of a man and a woman, where neither party owes child support or is in prison." Nor did the interracial marriage ban at issue in Loving define marriage as "the union of a man and a woman of the same race." See Tragen, *Comment, Statutory Prohibitions Against Interracial Marriage*, 32 Cal. L. Rev. 269 (1944) ("at common law there was no ban on interracial marriage"); post, at 11–12, n. 5 (THOMAS, J., dissenting). Removing racial barriers to marriage therefore did not change what a marriage was any more than integrating schools changed what a school was. As the majority admits, the institution of "marriage" discussed in every one of these cases "presumed a relationship involving opposite-sex partners." *Ante*, at 11.

In short, the "right to marry" cases stand for the important but limited proposition that particular restrictions on access to marriage as *traditionally defined* violate due process. These precedents say nothing at all about a right to make a State change its definition of marriage, which is the right petitioners actually seek here. See *Windsor*, 570 U.S., at ___ (ALITO, J., dissenting) (slip op., at 8) ("What Windsor and the United States seek ... is not the protection of a deeply rooted right but the recognition of a very new right."). Neither petitioners nor the majority cites a single case or other legal source providing any basis for such a constitutional right. None exists, and that is enough to foreclose their claim.

2

The majority suggests that "there are other, more instructive precedents" informing the right to marry. Ante, at 12. Although not entirely clear, this reference seems to correspond to a line of cases discussing an implied fundamental "right of privacy." *Griswold*, 381 U.S., at 486. In the first of those cases, the Court invalidated a criminal law that banned the use of contraceptives. Id., at 485–486. The Court stressed the invasive nature of the ban, which threatened the intrusion of "the police to search the sacred precincts of marital bedrooms." Id., at 485. In the Court's view, such laws infringed the right to privacy in its most basic sense: the "right to be let alone." *Eisenstadt v. Baird*, 405 U.S. 438, 453–454, n. 10 (1972) (internal quotation marks omitted); see *Olmstead v. United States*, 277 U.S. 438, 478 (1928) (Brandeis, J., dissenting).

The Court also invoked the right to privacy in *Lawrence v. Texas*, 539 U.S. 558 (2003), which struck down a Texas statute criminalizing homosexual sodomy. Lawrence relied on the position that criminal sodomy laws, like bans on contraceptives, invaded privacy by inviting "unwarranted government intrusions" that "touc[h] upon the most private human conduct, sexual behavior ... in the most private of places, the home." Id., at 562, 567.

Neither *Lawrence* nor any other precedent in the privacy line of cases supports the right that petitioners assert here. Unlike criminal laws banning contraceptives and sodomy, the marriage laws at issue here involve no government intrusion. They create no crime and impose no punishment. Same-sex couples remain free to live together,to engage in intimate conduct, and to raise their families as they see fit. No one is "condemned to live in loneliness" by the laws challenged in these cases—no one. Ante, at 28. At the same time, the laws in no way interfere with the "right to be let alone."

The majority also relies on Justice Harlan's influential dissenting opinion in *Poe v. Ullman*, 367 U.S. 497 (1961). As the majority recounts, that opinion states that "[d]ue process has not been reduced to any formula." Id., at 542. But far from conferring the broad interpretive discretion that the majority discerns, Justice Harlan's opinion makes clear that courts implying fundamental rights are not "free to roam where unguided speculation might take them." Ibid. They must instead have "regard to what history teaches" and exercise not only "judgment" but "restraint." Ibid. Of particular relevance, Justice Harlan explained that "laws regarding marriage which provide both when the sexual powers may be used and the legal and societal context in which children are born and brought up ... form a pattern so deeply pressed into the substance of our social life that any Constitutional doctrine in this area must build upon that basis." Id., at 546.

In sum, the privacy cases provide no support for the majority's position, because petitioners do not seek privacy. Quite the opposite, they seek public recognition of their relationships, along with corresponding government benefits. Our cases have consistently refused to allow litigants to convert the shield provided by constitutional liberties into a sword to demand positive entitlements from the State. See *DeShaney* v. *Winnebago County Dept. of Social Servs.*, 489 U.S. 189, 196 (1989); *San Antonio Independent School Dist.* v. *Rodriguez*, 411 U.S. 1, 35–37 (1973); post, at 9–13 (THOMAS, J., dissenting). Thus, although the right to privacy recognized by our precedents certainly plays a role in protecting the intimate conduct of same-sex couples, it provides no affirmative right to redefine marriage and no basis for striking down the laws a tissue here.

3

Perhaps recognizing how little support it can derive from precedent, the majority goes out of its way to jettison the "careful" approach to implied fundamental rights taken by this Court in *Glucksberg*. *Ante*, at 18 (quoting 521 U.S., at 721). It is revealing that the majority's position requires it to effectively overrule *Glucksberg*, the leading modern case setting the bounds of substantive due process. At least this part of the majority opinion has the virtue of candor. Nobody could rightly accuse the majority of taking a careful approach.

Ultimately, only one precedent offers any support for the majority's methodology: *Lochner* v. *New York*, 198 U.S. 45. The majority opens its opinion by announcing petitioners' right to "define and express their identity." *Ante*, at 1–2. The majority later explains that "the right to personal choice regarding marriage is inherent in the concept of individual autonomy." *Ante*, at 12. This freewheeling notion of individual autonomy echoes nothing so much as "the general right of an individual to be *free in his person* and in his power to contract in relation to his own labor." *Lochner*, 198 U.S., at 58 (emphasis added).

To be fair, the majority does not suggest that its individual autonomy right is entirely unconstrained. The constraints it sets are precisely those that accord with its own "reasoned judgment," informed by its "new insight" into the "nature of injustice," which was invisible to all who came before but has become clear "as we learn [the] meaning" of liberty. *Ante*, at 10, 11. The truth is that today's decision rests on nothing more than the majority's own conviction that same-sex couples should be allowed to marry because they want to, and that "it would disparage their choices and diminish their personhood to deny them this right." *Ante*, at 19. Whatever force that belief may have as a matter of moral philosophy, it has no more basis in the Constitution than did the naked policy preferences adopted in *Lochner*. See 198 U.S., at 61 ("We do not believe in the soundness of the views which uphold this law," which "is an illegal interference with the rights of individuals ... to make contracts regarding labor upon such terms as they may think best").

The majority recognizes that today's cases do not mark "the first time the Court has been asked to adopt a cautious approach to recognizing and protecting fundamental rights." *Ante*, at 25. On that much, we agree. The Court was "asked"—and it agreed—to "adopt a cautious approach" to implying fundamental rights after the debacle of the *Lochner* era. Today, the majority casts caution aside and revives the grave errors of that period.

One immediate question invited by the majority's position is whether States may retain the definition of marriage as a union of two people. Cf. *Brown v. Buhman*, 947 F. Supp. 2d 1170 (Utah 2013), appeal pending, No. 144117 (CA10). Although the majority randomly inserts the adjective "two" in various places, it offers no reason at all why the two-person element of the core definition of marriage may be preserved while the man-woman element may not. Indeed, from the standpoint of history and tradition, a leap from opposite-sex marriage to same-sex marriage is much greater than one from a two-person union to plural unions, which have deep roots in some cultures around the world. If the majority is willing to take the big leap, it is hard to see how it can say no to the shorter one.

It is striking how much of the majority's reasoning would apply with equal force to the claim of a fundamental right to plural marriage. If "[t]here is dignity in the bond between two men or two women who seek to marry and in their autonomy to make such profound choices," ante, at 13, why would there be any less dignity in the bond between three people who, in exercising their autonomy, seek to make the profound choice to marry? If a same-sex couple has the constitutional right to marry because their children would otherwise "suffer the stigma of knowing their families are somehow lesser," *ante*, at 15, why wouldn't the same reasoning apply to a family of three or more persons raising children? If not having the opportunity to marry "serves to disrespect and subordinate" gay and lesbian couples, why wouldn't the same "imposition of this disability," *ante*, at 22, serve to disrespect and subordinate people who find fulfillment in polyamorous relationships? See Bennett, Polyamory: The Next Sexual Revolution? Newsweek, July 28, 2009 (estimating 500,000 polyamorous families in the United States); Li, *Married Lesbian "Throuple"* Expecting First Child, *N. Y. Post*, Apr. 23, 2014; Otter, *Three May Not Be a Crowd: The Case for a Constitutional Right to Plural Marriage,* 64 Emory L. J.1977 (2015).

I do not mean to equate marriage between same-sex couples with plural marriages in all respects. There may well be relevant differences that compel different legal analysis. But if there are, petitioners have not pointed to any. When asked about a plural marital union at oral argument, petitioners asserted that a State "doesn't have such an institution." Tr. of Oral Arg. on Question 2, p. 6. But that is exactly the point: the States at issue here do not have an institution of same-sex marriage, either.

4

Near the end of its opinion, the majority offers perhaps the clearest insight into its decision. Expanding marriage to include same-sex couples, the majority insists, would "pose no risk of harm to themselves or third parties." *Ante*, at 27. This argument again echoes *Lochner*, which relied on its assessment that "we think that a law like the one before us involves neither the safety, the morals nor the welfare of the public, and that the interest of the public is not in the slightest degree affected by such an act." 198 U.S., at 57.

Then and now, this assertion of the "harm principle" sounds more in philosophy than law. The elevation of the fullest individual self-realization over the constraints that society has expressed in law may or may not be attractive moral philosophy. But a Justice's commission does not confer any special moral, philosophical, or social insight sufficient to justify imposing those perceptions on fellow citizens under the pretense of "due process." There is indeed a process due the people on issues of this sort—the democratic process. Respecting that understanding requires the Court to be guided by law, not any particular school of social thought. As Judge Henry Friendly once put it, echoing Justice Holmes's dissent in *Lochner*, the Fourteenth Amendment does not enact John Stuart Mill's On Liberty any more than it enacts *Herbert Spencer's Social Statics*. See Randolph, Before *Roe* v. *Wade*: Judge Friendly's Draft Abortion Opinion, 29 Harv. J. L. & Pub. Pol'y 1035, 1036–1037, 1058 (2006). And it certainly does not enact any one concept of marriage.

The majority's understanding of due process lays out a tantalizing vision of the future for Members of this Court: If an unvarying social institution enduring over all of recorded history cannot inhibit judicial policymaking, what can? But this approach is dangerous for the rule of law. The purpose of insisting that implied fundamental rights have roots in the history and tradition of our people is to ensure that when unelected judges strike down democratically enacted laws, they do so based on something more than their own beliefs. The Court today not only overlooks our country's entire history and tradition but actively repudiates it, preferring to live only in the heady days of the here and now. I agree with the majority that the "nature of injustice is that we may not always see it in our own times." *Ante*, at 11. As petitioners put it, "times can blind." Tr. of Oral Arg. on Question 1, at 9, 10. But to blind yourself to history is both prideful and unwise. "The past is never dead. It's not even past." W. Faulkner, *Requiem for a Nun* 92 (1951).

III

In addition to their due process argument, petitioners contend that the Equal Protection Clause requires their States to license and recognize same-sex marriages. The majority does not seriously engage with this claim. Its discussion is, quite frankly, difficult to follow. The central point seems to be that there is a "synergy between" the *Equal Protection Clause* and the *Due Process Clause*, and that some precedents relying on one Clause have also relied on the other. *Ante*, at 20. Absent from this portion of the opinion, however, is anything resembling our usual framework for deciding equal protection cases. It is casebook doctrine that the "modern Supreme Court's treatment of equal protection claims has used a means-ends methodology in which judges ask whether the classification the government is using is sufficiently related to the goals it is pursuing." G. Stone, L. Seidman, C. Sunstein, M. Tushnet, & P. Karlan, *Constitutional Law* 453 (7th ed. 2013). The majority's approach today is different:

> "Rights implicit in liberty and rights secured by equal protection may rest on different precepts and are not always co-extensive, yet in some instances each maybe instructive as to the meaning and reach of the other. In any particular case one Clause may be thought to capture the essence of the right in a more accurate and comprehensive way, even as the two Clauses may converge in the identification and definition of the right." *Ante*, at 19.

The majority goes on to assert in conclusory fashion that the *Equal Protection Clause* provides an alternative basis for its holding. Ante, at 22. Yet the majority fails to provide even a single sentence explaining how the *Equal Protection Clause* supplies independent weight for its position, nor does it attempt to justify its gratuitous violation of the canon against unnecessarily resolving constitutional questions. See *Northwest Austin Municipal Util. Dist. No. One* v. *Holder*, 557 U.S. 193, 197 (2009). In any event, the marriage laws at issue here do not violate the

Equal Protection Clause, because distinguishing between opposite-sex and same-sex couples is rationally related to the States' "legitimate state interest" in "preserving the traditional institution of marriage." *Lawrence*, 539 U.S., at 585 (O'Connor, J., concurring in judgment).

It is important to note with precision which laws petitioners have challenged. Although they discuss some of the ancillary legal benefits that accompany marriage, such as hospital visitation rights and recognition of spousal status on official documents, petitioners' lawsuits target the laws defining marriage generally rather than those allocating benefits specifically. The equal protection analysis might be different, in my view, if we were confronted with a more focused challenge to the denial of certain tangible benefits. Of course, those more selective claims will not arise now that the Court has taken the drastic step of requiring every State to license and recognize marriages between same-sex couples.

IV

The legitimacy of this Court ultimately rests "upon the respect accorded to its judgments." Republican Party of Minn. v. White, 536 U.S. 765, 793 (2002) (KENNEDY, J., concurring). That respect flows from the perception—and reality—that we exercise humility and restraint in deciding cases according to the Constitution and law. The role of the Court envisioned by the majority today, however, is anything but humble or restrained. Over and over, the majority exalts the role of the judiciary in delivering social change. In the majority's telling, it is the courts, not the people, who are responsible for making "new dimensions of freedom ... apparent to new generations," for providing "formal discourse" on social issues, and for ensuring "neutral discussions, without scornful or disparaging commentary." *Ante*, at 7–9.

Nowhere is the majority's extravagant conception of judicial supremacy more evident than in its description—and dismissal—of the public debate regarding same-sex marriage. Yes, the majority concedes, on one side are thousands of years of human history in every society known to have populated the planet. But on the other side, there has been "extensive litigation," "many thoughtful District Court decisions," "countless studies, papers, books, and other popular and scholarly writings," and "more than 100" *amicus* briefs in these cases alone. *Ante*, at 9, 10, 23. What would be the point of allowing the democratic process to go on? It is high time for the Court to decide the meaning of marriage, based on five lawyers' "better informed understanding" of "a liberty that remains urgent in our own era." *Ante*, at 19. The answer is surely there in one of those amicus briefs or studies.

Those who founded our country would not recognize the majority's conception of the judicial role. They after all risked their lives and fortunes for the precious right to govern themselves. They would never have imagined yielding that right on a question of social policy to unaccountable and unelected judges. And they certainly would not have been satisfied by a system empowering judges to override policy judgments so long as they do so after "a quite extensive discussion." *Ante*, at 8. In our democracy, debate about the content of the law is not an exhaustion requirement to be checked off before courts can impose their will. "Surely the Constitution does not put either the legislative branch or the executive branch in the position of a television quiz show contestant so that when a given period of time has elapsed and a problem remains unresolved by them, the federal judiciary may press a buzzer and take its turn at fashioning a solution." Rehnquist, *The Notion of a Living Constitution,* 54 Texas L. Rev. 693,700 (1976). As a plurality of this Court explained just last year, "It is demeaning to the democratic process to presume that voters are not capable of deciding an issue of this sensitivity on decent and rational grounds." *Schuette* v. *BAMN*, 572 U.S. ___, ___ –___ (2014) (slip op., at 16– 17).

The Court's accumulation of power does not occur in a vacuum. It comes at the expense of the people. And they know it. Here and abroad, people are in the midst of a serious and thoughtful public debate on the issue of same-sex marriage. They see voters carefully considering same-sex marriage, casting ballots in favor or opposed, and sometimes changing their minds. They see political leaders similarly reexamining their positions, and either reversing course or explaining adherence to old convictions confirmed anew. They see governments and businesses modifying policies and practices with respect to same-sex couples, and participating actively in the civic discourse. They see countries overseas democratically accepting profound social change, or declining to do so. This deliberative process is making people take seriously questions that they may not have even regarded as questions before.

When decisions are reached through democratic means, some people will inevitably be disappointed with the results. But those whose views do not prevail at least know that they have had their say, and accordingly are—in the tradition of our political culture—reconciled to the result of a fair and honest debate. In addition, they can gear up to raise the issue later, hoping to persuade enough on the winning side to think again. "That is exactly how our system of government is supposed to work." Post, at 2–3 (SCALIA, J., dissenting).

But today the Court puts a stop to all that. By deciding this question under the Constitution, the Court removes it from the realm of democratic decision. There will be consequences to shutting down the political process on an issue of such profound public significance. Closing debate tends to close minds. People denied a voice are less likely to accept the ruling of a court on an issue that does not seem to be the sort of thing courts usually decide. As a thoughtful commentator observed about another issue, "The political process was moving..., not swiftly enough for advocates of quick, complete change, but majoritarian institutions were listening and acting. Heavy-handed judicial intervention was difficult to justify and appears to have provoked, not resolved, conflict." Ginsburg, Some Thoughts on Autonomy and Equality in Relation to *Roe* v. *Wade*, 63 N. C. L. Rev. 375, 385–386 (1985) (footnote omitted). Indeed, however heartened the proponents of same-sex marriage might be on this day, it is worth acknowledging what they have lost, and lost forever: the opportunity to win the true acceptance that comes from persuading their fellow citizens of the justice of their cause. And they lose this just when the winds of change were freshening at their backs.

Federal courts are blunt instruments when it comes to creating rights. They have constitutional power only to resolve concrete cases or controversies; they do not have the flexibility of legislatures to address concerns of parties not before the court or to anticipate problems that may arise from the exercise of a new right. Today's decision, for example, creates serious questions about religious liberty. Many good and decent people oppose same-sex marriage as a tenet of faith, and their freedom to exercise religion is—unlike the right imagined by the majority—actually spelled out in the Constitution. Amdt. 1.

Respect for sincere religious conviction has led voters and legislators in every State that has adopted same-sex marriage democratically to include accommodations for religious practice. The majority's decision imposing same-sex marriage cannot, of course, create any such accommodations. The majority graciously suggests that religious believers may continue to "advocate" and "teach" their views of marriage.

Ante, at 27. The First Amendment guarantees, however, the freedom to "*exercise*" religion. Ominously, that is not a word the majority uses.

Hard questions arise when people of faith exercise religion in ways that may be seen to conflict with the new right to same-sex marriage—when, for example, a religious college provides married student housing only to opposite-sex married couples, or a religious adoption agency declines to place children with same-sex married couples. Indeed, the Solicitor General candidly acknowledged that the tax exemptions of some religious institutions would be in question if they opposed same-sex marriage. See Tr. of Oral Arg. on Question 1, at 36–38. There is little doubt that these and similar questions will soon be before this Court. Unfortunately, people of faith can take no comfort in the treatment they receive from the majority today.

Perhaps the most discouraging aspect of today's decision is the extent to which the majority feels compelled to sully those on the other side of the debate. The majority offers a cursory assurance that it does not intend to disparage people who, as a matter of conscience, cannot accept same-sex marriage. Ante, at 19. That disclaimer is hard to square with the very next sentence, in which the majority explains that "the necessary consequence" of laws codifying the traditional definition of marriage is to "demea[n] or stigmatiz[e]" same-sex couples. *Ante*, at 19. The majority reiterates such characterizations over and over. By the majority's account, Americans who did nothing more than follow the understanding of marriage that has existed for our entire history—in particular, the tens of millions of people who voted to reaffirm their States' enduring definition of marriage—have acted to "lock ... out," "disparage,""disrespect and subordinate," and inflict "[d]ignitary wounds" upon their gay and lesbian neighbors. *Ante*, at 17, 19, 22, 25. These apparent assaults on the character of fair-minded people will have an effect, in society and in court. See post, at 6–7 (ALITO, J., dissenting). Moreover, they are entirely gratuitous. It is one thing for the majority to conclude that the Constitution protects a right to same-sex marriage; it is something else to portray everyone who does not share the majority's "better informed understanding" as bigoted. *Ante*, at 19.

In the face of all this, a much different view of the Court's role is possible. That view is more modest and restrained. It is more skeptical that the legal abilities of judges also reflect insight into moral and philosophical issues. It is more sensitive to the fact that judges are unelected and unaccountable, and that the legitimacy of their power depends on confining it to the exercise of legal judgment. It is more attuned to the lessons of history, and what it has meant for the country and Court when Justices have exceeded their proper bounds. And it is less pretentious than to suppose that while people around the world have viewed an institution in a particular way for thousands of years, the present generation and the present Court are the ones chosen to burst the bonds of that history and tradition.

* * *

If you are among the many Americans—of whatever sexual orientation—who favor expanding same-sex marriage, by all means celebrate today's decision. Celebrate the achievement of a desired goal. Celebrate the opportunity for a new expression of commitment to a partner. Celebrate the availability of new benefits. But do not celebrate the Constitution. It had nothing to do with it.

I respectfully dissent.

Threat To Democracy
Justice Antonin Scalia

JUSTICE SCALIA, with whom JUSTICE THOMAS joins, dissenting.

The substance of today's decree is not of immense personal importance to me. The law can recognize as marriage whatever sexual attachments and living arrangements it wishes, and can accord them favorable civil consequences, from tax treatment to rights of inheritance. Those civil consequences—and the public approval that conferring the name of marriage evidences—can perhaps have adverse social effects, but no more adverse than the effects of many other controversial laws. So it is not of special importance to me what the law says about marriage. It is of overwhelming importance, however, who it is that rules me. Today's decree says that my Ruler, and the Ruler of 320 million Americans coast-to-coast, is a majority of the nine lawyers on the Supreme Court. The opinion in these cases is the furthest extension in fact—and the furthest extension one can even imagine—of the Court's claimed power to create "liberties" that the Constitution and its Amendments neglect to mention. This practice of constitutional revision by an unelected committee of nine, always accompanied (as it is today) by extravagant praise of liberty, robs the People of the most important liberty they asserted in the Declaration of Independence and won in the Revolution of 1776: the freedom to govern themselves.

I

Until the courts put a stop to it, public debate over same-sex marriage displayed American democracy at its best. Individuals on both sides of the issue passionately, but respectfully, attempted to persuade their fellow citizens to accept their views. Americans considered the arguments and put the question to a vote. The electorates of 11 States, either directly or through their representatives, chose to expand the traditional definition of marriage. Many more decided not to.[16] Win or lose, advocates for both sides continued pressing their cases, secure in the knowledge that an electoral loss can be negated by a later electoral win. That is exactly how our system of government is supposed to work.[17]

The Constitution places some constraints on self-rule—constraints adopted by the People themselves when they ratified the Constitution and its Amendments. Forbidden are laws "impairing the Obligation of Contracts,"[18] denying "Full Faith and Credit" to the "public Acts" of other States,[19] prohibiting the free exercise of religion,[20] abridging the freedom of speech,[21] infringing the right to keep and bear arms,[22] authorizing unreasonable searches and seizures,[23] and so forth. Aside from these limitations, those powers "reserved to the States respectively, or to the people"[24] can be exercised as the States or the People desire. These cases ask us to decide whether the Fourteenth Amendment contains a limitation that requires the States to license and recognize marriages between two people of the same sex. Does it remove that issue from the political process?

Of course not. It would be surprising to find a prescription regarding marriage in the Federal Constitution since, as the author of today's opinion reminded us only two years ago (in an opinion joined by the same Justices who join him today):

> "[R]egulation of domestic relations is an area that has long been regarded as a virtually exclusive province of the States."[25]

> "[T]he Federal Government, through our history, has deferred to state-law policy decisions with respect to domestic relations."[26]

But we need not speculate. When the Fourteenth Amendment was ratified in 1868, every State limited marriage to one man and one woman, and no one doubted the constitutionality of doing so. That resolves these cases. When it comes to determining the meaning of a vague constitutional provision—such as "due process of law" or "equal protection of the laws"—it is unquestionable that the People who ratified that provision did not understand it to prohibit a practice that remained both universal and uncontroversial in the years after ratification.[27] We have no basis for striking down a practice that is not expressly prohibited by the Fourteenth Amendment's text, and that bears the endorsement of a long tradition of open, widespread, and unchallenged use dating back to the Amendment's ratification. Since there is no doubt whatever that the People never decided to prohibit the limitation of marriage to opposite-sex couples, the public debate over same-sex marriage must be allowed to continue.

But the Court ends this debate, in an opinion lacking even a thin veneer of law. Buried beneath the mummeries and straining-to-be-memorable passages of the opinion is a candid and startling assertion: No matter what it was the People ratified, the Fourteenth Amendment protects those rights that the Judiciary, in its "reasoned judgment," thinks the Fourteenth Amendment ought to protect.[28] That is so because "[t]he generations that wrote and ratified the Bill of Rights and the Fourteenth Amendment did not presume to know the extent of freedom in all of its dimensions .... "[29] One would think that sentence would continue: "... and therefore they provided for a means by which the People could amend the Constitution," or perhaps "... and therefore they left the creation of additional liberties, such as the freedom to marry someone of the same sex, to the People, through the never-ending process of legislation." But no. What logically follows, in the majority's judge-empowering estimation, is: "and so they entrusted to future generations a charter protecting the right of all persons to enjoy liberty as we learn its meaning."[30] The "we," needless to say, is the nine of us. "History and tradition guide and discipline [our] inquiry but do not set its outer boundaries."[31] Thus, rather than focusing on the People's understanding of "liberty"—at the time of ratification or even today—the majority focuses on four "principles and traditions" that, in the majority's view, prohibit States from defining marriage as an institution consisting of one man and one woman.[32]

This is a naked judicial claim to legislative—indeed, super-legislative—power; a claim fundamentally at odds with our system of government. Except as limited by a constitutional prohibition agreed to by the People, the States are free to adopt whatever laws they like, even those that offend the esteemed Justices' "reasoned judgment." A system of government that makes the People subordinate to a committee of nine unelected lawyers does not deserve to be called a democracy.

Judges are selected precisely for their skill as lawyers; whether they reflect the policy views of a particular constituency is not (or should not be) relevant. Not surprisingly then, the Federal Judiciary is hardly a cross-section of America. Take, for example, this Court, which consists of only nine men and women, all of them successful lawyers[33] who studied at Harvard or Yale Law School. Four of the nine are natives of New York City. Eight of them grew up in east- and west-coast States. Only one hails from the vast expanse in-between. Not a single South-westerner or even, to tell the truth, a genuine Westerner (California does not count). Not a single evangelical Christian (a group that comprises about one quarter of Americans [34]), or even a Protestant of any denomination. The strikingly unrepresentative character of the body voting on today's social upheaval would be irrelevant if they were functioning as judges, answering the legal question whether the

American people had ever ratified a constitutional provision that was understood to proscribe the traditional definition of marriage. But of course the Justices in today's majority are not voting on that basis; they say they are not. And to allow the policy question of same-sex marriage to be considered and resolved by a select, patrician, highly unrepresentative panel of nine is to violate a principle even more fundamental than no taxation without representation: no social transformation without representation.

II

But what really astounds is the hubris reflected in today's judicial Putsch. The five Justices who compose today's majority are entirely comfortable concluding that every State violated the Constitution for all of the 135 years between the Fourteenth Amendment's ratification and Massachusetts' permitting of same-sex marriages in 2003.[35] They have discovered in the Fourteenth Amendment a "fundamental right" overlooked by every person alive at the time of ratification, and almost everyone else in the time since. They see what lesser legal minds—minds like Thomas Cooley, John Marshall Harlan, Oliver Wendell Holmes, Jr., Learned Hand, Louis Brandeis, William Howard Taft, Benjamin Cardozo, Hugo Black, Felix Frankfurter, Robert Jackson, and Henry Friendly—could not. They are certain that the People ratified the Fourteenth Amendment to bestow on them the power to remove questions from the democratic process when that is called for by their "reasoned judgment." These Justices know that limiting marriage to one man and one woman is contrary to reason; they know that an institution as old as government itself, and accepted by every nation in history until 15 years ago,[36] cannot possibly be supported by anything other than ignorance or bigotry. And they are willing to say that any citizen who does not agree with that, who adheres to what was, until 15 years ago, the unanimous judgment of all generations and all societies, stands against the Constitution.

The opinion is couched in a style that is as pretentious as its content is egotistic. It is one thing for separate concurring or dissenting opinions to contain extravagances, even silly extravagances, of thought and expression; it is something else for the official opinion of the Court to do so.[37] Of course the opinion's showy profundities are often profoundly incoherent. "The nature of marriage is that, through its enduring bond, two persons together can find other freedoms, such as expression, intimacy, and spirituality."[38] (Really? Who ever thought that intimacy and spirituality [whatever that means] were freedoms? And if intimacy is, one would think Freedom of Intimacy is abridged rather than expanded by marriage. Ask the nearest hippie. Expression, sure enough, is a freedom, but anyone in a long-lasting marriage will attest that that happy state constricts, rather than expands, what one can prudently say.) Rights, we are told, can "rise ... from a better informed understanding of how constitutional imperatives define a liberty that remains urgent in our own era."[39] (Huh? How can a better informed understanding of how constitutional imperatives [whatever that means] define [whatever that means] an urgent liberty [never mind], give birth to a right?) And we are told that, "[i]n any particular case," either the Equal Protection or Due Process Clause "may be thought to capture the essence of [a] right in a more accurate and comprehensive way," than the other, "even as the two Clauses may converge in the identification and definition of the right."[40] (What say? What possible "essence" does substantive due process "capture" in an "accurate and comprehensive way"? It stands for nothing whatever, except those freedoms and entitlements that this Court really likes. And the Equal Protection Clause, as employed today, identifies nothing except a difference in treatment that this Court *really* dislikes. Hardly a distillation of essence. If the opinion is correct that the two clauses "converge in the identification and definition of [a] right," that is only because the majority's likes and dislikes are predictably compatible.) I could go on. The world does not expect logic and precision in poetry or inspirational pop-philosophy; it demands them in the law. The stuff contained in today's opinion has to diminish this Court's reputation for clear thinking and sober analysis.

* * *

Hubris is sometimes defined as o'erweening pride; and pride, we know, goeth before a fall. The Judiciary is the "least dangerous" of the federal branches because it has "neither Force nor Will, but merely judgment; and must ultimately depend upon the aid of the executive arm" and the

States, "even for the efficacy of its judgments."[41] With each decision of ours that takes from the People a question properly left to them—with each decision that is unabashedly based not on law, but on the "reasoned judgment" of a bare majority of this Court—we move one step closer to being reminded of our impotence.

Inestimable Consequences
Justice Clarence Thomas

JUSTICE THOMAS, with whom JUSTICE SCALIA joins, dissenting.

The Court's decision today is at odds not only with the Constitution, but with the principles upon which our Nation was built. Since well before 1787, liberty has been understood as freedom from government action, not entitlement to government benefits. The Framers created our Constitution to preserve that understanding of liberty. Yet the majority invokes our Constitution in the name of a "liberty" that the Framers would not have recognized, to the detriment of the liberty they sought to protect. Along the way, it rejects the idea—captured in our Declaration of Independence—that human dignity is innate and suggests instead that it comes from the Government. This distortion of our Constitution not only ignores the text, it inverts the relationship between the individual and the state in our Republic. I cannot agree with it.

I

The majority's decision today will require States to issue marriage licenses to same-sex couples and to recognize same-sex marriages entered in other States largely based on a constitutional provision guaranteeing "due process" before a person is deprived of his "life, liberty, or property." I have elsewhere explained the dangerous fiction of treating the Due Process Clause as a font of substantive rights. *McDonald* v. *Chicago*, 561 U.S. 742, 811–812 (2010) (THOMAS, J., concurring in part and concurring in judgment). It distorts the constitutional text, which guarantees only whatever "process" is "due" before a person is deprived of life, liberty, and property. U.S. Const., Amdt. 14, §1. Worse, it invites judges to do exactly what the majority has done here—"'roa[m] at large in the constitutional field' guided only by their personal views" as to the "'fundamental rights'" protected by that document. *Planned Parenthood of Southeastern Pa.* v. *Casey*, 505 U.S. 833, 953, 965 (1992) (Rehnquist, C. J., concurring in judgment in part and dissenting in part) (quoting *Griswold* v. *Connecticut*, 381 U.S. 479, 502 (1965) (Harlan, J., concurring in judgment)).

By straying from the text of the Constitution, substantive due process exalts judges at the expense of the People from whom they derive their authority. Petitioners argue that by enshrining the traditional definition of marriage in their State Constitutions through voter-approved amendments, the States have put the issue "beyond the reach of the normal democratic process." Brief for Petitioners in No. 14–562, p. 54. But the result petitioners seek is far less democratic. They ask nine judges on this Court to enshrine their definition of marriage in the Federal Constitution and thus put it beyond the reach of the normal democratic process for the entire Nation. That a "bare majority" of this Court, *ante*, at 25, is able to grant this wish, wiping out with a stroke of the keyboard the results of the political process in over 30 States, based on a provision that guarantees only "due process" is but further evidence of the danger of substantive due process.[42]

II

Even if the doctrine of substantive due process were somehow defensible—it is not—petitioners still would not have a claim. To invoke the protection of the Due Process Clause at all—whether under a theory of "substantive" or "procedural" due process—a party must first identify a deprivation of "life, liberty, or property." The majority claims these state laws deprive petitioners of "liberty," but the concept of "liberty" it conjures up bears no resemblance to any plausible meaning of that word as it is used in the Due Process Clauses.

A

1

As used in the Due Process Clauses, "liberty" most likely refers to "the power of loco-motion, of changing situation, or removing one's person to whatsoever place one's own inclination may direct; without imprisonment or restraint, unless by due course of law." 1 W. Blackstone, *Commentaries on the Laws of England* 130 (1769) (Blackstone). That definition is drawn from the historical roots of the Clauses and is consistent with our Constitution's text and structure.

Both of the Constitution's *Due Process Clauses* reach back to *Magna Carta*. See *Davidson* v. *New Orleans*, 96 U.S. 97, 101–102 (1878). Chapter 39 of the original *Magna Carta* provided, "No free man shall be taken, imprisoned, disseised, outlawed, banished, or in any way destroyed, nor will We proceed against or prosecute him, except by the lawful judgment of his peers and by the law of the land." *Magna Carta*, ch. 39, in A. Howard, *Magna Carta*: Text and Commentary 43 (1964). Although the 1215 version of *Magna Carta* was in effect for only a few weeks, this provision was later reissued in 1225 with modest changes to its wording as follows: "No freeman shall be taken, or imprisoned, or be disseised of his freehold, or liberties, or free customs, or be outlawed, or exiled, or any otherwise destroyed; nor will we not pass upon him, nor condemn him, but by lawful judgment of his peers or by the law of the land." 1 E. Coke, The Second Part of the *Institutes of the Laws of England* 45 (1797). In his influential commentary on the provision many years later, Sir Edward Coke interpreted the words "by the law of the land" to mean the same thing as "by due proces of the common law." Id., at 50.

After *Magna Carta* became subject to renewed interest in the 17th century, see, e.g., ibid., William Blackstone referred to this provision as protecting the "absolute rights of every Englishman." 1 Blackstone 123. And he formulated those absolute rights as "the right of personal security," which included the right to life; "the right of personal liberty"; and "the right of private property." Id., at 125. He defined "the right of personal liberty" as "the power of loco-motion, of changing situation, or removing one's person to whatsoever place one's own inclination may direct; without imprisonment or restraint, unless by due course of law." Id., at 125, 130.[43]

The Framers drew heavily upon Blackstone's formulation, adopting provisions in early State Constitutions that replicated *Magna Carta's* language, but were modified to refer specifically to "life, liberty, or property."[44] State decisions interpreting these provisions between the founding and the ratification of the Fourteenth Amendment almost uniformly construed the word "liberty" to refer only to freedom from physical restraint. See Warren, *The New "Liberty" Under the Fourteenth Amendment,* 39 Harv. L. Rev. 431, 441–445 (1926). Even one case that has been identified as a possible exception to that view merely used broad language about liberty in the context of a habeas corpus proceeding—a proceeding classically associated with obtaining freedom from physical restraint. Cf. id., at 444–445.

In enacting the Fifth Amendment's *Due Process Clause,* the Framers similarly chose to employ the "life, liberty, or property" formulation, though they otherwise deviated substantially from the States' use of *Magna Carta's* language in the Clause. See Shattuck, The True Meaning of the Term "Liberty" in Those Clauses in the Federal and State Constitutions Which Protect "Life, Liberty, and Property," 4 Harv. L. Rev. 365, 382 (1890). When read in light of the history of that formulation, it is hard to see how the "liberty" protected by the Clause could be interpreted to include anything broader than freedom from physical restraint. That was the consistent usage of the time when "liberty" was paired with "life" and "property."See id., at 375. And that usage avoids rendering superfluous those protections for "life" and "property."

If the Fifth Amendment uses "liberty" in this narrow sense, then the Fourteenth Amendment likely does as well. See *Hurtado v. California,* 110 U.S. 516, 534–535 (1884). Indeed, this Court has previously commented, "The conclusion is ... irresistible, that when the same phrase was employed in the Fourteenth Amendment [as was used in the Fifth Amendment], it was used in the same sense and with no greater extent." Ibid. And this Court's earliest Fourteenth Amendment decisions appear to interpret the Clause as using "liberty" to mean freedom from physical restraint. In *Munn* v. *Illinois*, 94 U.S. 113 (1877), for example, the Court recognized the relationship between the two Due Process Clauses and *Magna Carta*, see id., at 123–124, and implicitly rejected the dissent's argument that "'liberty'" encompassed "something more ... than mere freedom from physical restraint or the bounds of a prison," id., at 142 (Field, J., dissenting). That the Court appears to have lost its way in more recent years does not justify deviating from the original meaning of the Clauses.

2

Even assuming that the "liberty" in those Clauses encompasses something more than freedom from physical restraint, it would not include the types of rights claimed by the majority. In the American legal tradition, liberty has long been understood as individual freedom *from* governmental action, not as a right *to* a particular governmental entitlement.

The founding-era understanding of liberty was heavily influenced by John Locke, whose writings "on natural rights and on the social and governmental contract" were cited "[i]n pamphlet after pamphlet" by American writers. B. Bailyn, The Ideological Origins of the American Revolution 27 (1967). Locke described men as existing in a state of nature, possessed of the "perfect freedom to order their actions and dispose of their possessions and persons as they think fit, within the bounds of the law of nature, without asking leave, or depending upon the will of any other man." J. Locke, *Second Treatise of Civil Government,* §4, p. 4 (J. Gough ed. 1947) (Locke). Because that state of nature left men insecure in their persons and property, they entered civil society, trading a portion of their natural liberty for an increase in their security. See id., §97, at 49. Upon consenting to that order, men obtained civil liberty, or the freedom "to be under no other legislative power but that established by consent in the commonwealth; nor under the dominion of any will or restraint of any law, but what that legislative shall enact according to the trust put in it." Id., §22, at 13.[45]

This philosophy permeated the 18th-century political scene in America. A 1756 editorial in the Boston Gazette, for example, declared that

"Liberty in the *State of Nature*" was the "inherent natural Right" "of each Man" "to make a free Use of his Reason and Understanding, and to chuse that Action which he thinks he can give the best Account of," but that, "in Society, every Man parts with a Small Share of his natural Liberty, or lodges it in the publick Stock, that he may possess the Remainder without Controul." Boston Gazette and Country Journal, No. 58, May 10, 1756, p. 1. Similar sentiments were expressed in public speeches, sermons, and letters of the time. See 1 C. Hyneman & D. Lutz, American Political Writing During the Founding Era 1760–1805, pp. 100, 308, 385 (1983).

The founding-era idea of civil liberty as natural liberty constrained by human law necessarily involved only those freedoms that existed *outside* of government. See Hamburger, Natural Rights, Natural Law, and American Constitutions, 102 Yale L. J. 907, 918–919 (1993). As one later commentator observed, "[L]iberty in the eighteenth century was thought of much more in relation to 'negative liberty'; that is, freedom *from*, not freedom *to*, freedom from a number of social and political evils, including arbitrary government power." J. Reid, The Concept of Liberty in the Age of the American Revolution 56 (1988). Or as one scholar put it in 1776, "[T]he common idea of liberty is merely negative, and is only the absence of restraint." R. Hey, *Observations on the Nature of Civil Liberty and the Principles of Government* §13, p. 8 (1776) (Hey). When the colonists described laws that would infringe their liberties, they discussed laws that would prohibit individuals "from walking in the streets and highways on certain saints days, or from being abroad after a certain time in the evening, or ... restrain [them] from working up and manufacturing materials of [their] own growth." Downer, A Discourse at the Dedication of the Tree of Liberty, in 1 Hyneman, *supra*, at 101. Each of those examples involved freedoms that existed outside of government.

B

Whether we define "liberty" as locomotion or freedom from governmental action more broadly, petitioners have in no way been deprived of it. Petitioners cannot claim, under the most plausible definition of "liberty," that they have been imprisoned or physically restrained by the States for participating in same-sex relationships. To the contrary, they have been able to cohabitate and raise their children in peace. They have been able to hold civil marriage ceremonies in States that recognize same-sex marriages and private religious ceremonies in all States. They have been able to travel freely around the country, making their homes where they please. Far from being incarcerated or physically restrained, petitioners have been left alone to order their lives as they see fit.

Nor, under the broader definition, can they claim that the States have restricted their ability to go about their daily lives as they would be able to absent governmental restrictions. Petitioners do not ask this Court to order the States to stop restricting their ability to enter same-sex relationships, to engage in intimate behavior, to make vows to their partners in public ceremonies, to engage in religious wedding ceremonies, to hold themselves out as married, or to raise children. The States have imposed no such restrictions. Nor have the States prevented petitioners from approximating a number of incidents of marriage through private legal means, such as wills, trusts, and powers of attorney.

Instead, the States have refused to grant them governmental entitlements. Petitioners claim that as a matter of "liberty," they are entitled to access privileges and benefits that exist solely because of the government. They want, for example, to receive the State's imprimatur on their marriages—on state issued marriage licenses, death certificates, or other official forms. And they want to receive various monetary benefits, including reduced inheritance taxes upon the death of a spouse, compensation if a spouse dies as a result of a work-related injury, or loss of consortium damages in tort suits. But receiving governmental recognition and benefits has nothing to do with any understanding of "liberty" that the Framers would have recognized.

To the extent that the Framers would have recognized a natural right to marriage that fell within the broader definition of liberty, it would not have included a right to governmental recognition and benefits. Instead, it would have included a right to engage in the very same activities that petitioners have been left free to engage in—making vows, holding religious ceremonies celebrating those vows, raising children, and otherwise enjoying the society of one's spouse—without governmental interference. At the founding, such conduct was understood to predate government, not to flow from it. As Locke had explained many years earlier, "The first society was between man and wife, which gave beginning to that between parents and children." Locke §77, at 39; see also J. Wilson, *Lectures on Law*, in 2 Collected Works of James Wilson 1068

(K. Hall and M. Hall eds. 2007) (concluding "that to the institution of marriage the true origin of society must be traced"). Petitioners misunderstand the institution of marriage when they say that it would "mean little" absent governmental recognition. Brief for Petitioners in No. 14– 556, p. 33.

Petitioners' misconception of liberty carries over into their discussion of our precedents identifying a right to marry, not one of which has expanded the concept of "liberty" beyond the concept of negative liberty. Those precedents all involved absolute prohibitions on private actions associated with marriage. *Loving* v. *Virginia,* 388 U.S. 1 (1967), for example, involved a couple who was criminally prosecuted for marrying in the District of Columbia and cohabiting in Virginia, id., at 2–3.[46] They were each sentenced to a year of imprisonment, suspended for a term of 25 years on the condition that they not reenter the Commonwealth together during that time. Id., at 3.[47] In a similar vein, *Zablocki* v. *Redhail,* 434 U.S. 374 (1978), involved a man who was prohibited, on pain of criminal penalty, from "marry[ing] in Wisconsin or elsewhere" because of his outstanding child-support obligations, id., at 387; see id., at 377–378. And *Turner* v. *Safley*, 482 U.S. 78 (1987), involved state inmates who were prohibited from entering marriages without the permission of the superintendent of the prison, permission that could not be granted absent compelling reasons, id., at 82. In none of those cases were individuals denied solely governmental recognition and benefits associated with marriage.

In a concession to petitioners' misconception of liberty, the majority characterizes petitioners' suit as a quest to "find ... liberty by marrying someone of the same sex and having their marriages deemed lawful on the same terms and conditions as marriages between persons of the opposite sex." Ante, at 2. But "liberty" is not lost, nor can it be found in the way petitioners seek. As a philosophical matter, liberty is only freedom from governmental action, not an entitlement to governmental benefits. And as a constitutional matter, it is likely even narrower than that, encompassing only freedom from physical restraint and imprisonment. The majority's "better informed understanding of how constitutional imperatives define ... liberty," *ante*, at 19,—better informed, we must assume, than that of the people who ratified the Fourteenth Amendment—runs headlong into the reality that our Constitution is a "collection of 'Thou shalt nots,'" *Reid* v. *Covert*, 354 U.S. 1, 9 (1957) (plurality opinion), not "Thou shalt provides."

III

The majority's inversion of the original meaning of liberty will likely cause collateral damage to other aspects of our constitutional order that protect liberty.

A

The majority apparently disregards the political process as a protection for liberty. Although men, in forming a civil society, "give up all the power necessary to the ends for which they unite into society, to the majority of the community," Locke §99, at 49, they reserve the authority to exercise natural liberty within the bounds of laws established by that society, id., §22, at 13; see also Hey §§52, 54, at 30–32. To protect that liberty from arbitrary interference, they establish a process by which that society can adopt and enforce its laws. In our country, that process is primarily representative government at the state level, with the Federal Constitution serving as a backstop for that process. As a general matter, when the States act through their representative governments or by popular vote, the liberty of their residents is fully vindicated. This is no less true when some residents disagree with the result; indeed, it seems difficult to imagine any law on which all residents of a State would agree. See Locke §98, at 49 (suggesting that society would cease to function if it required unanimous consent to laws). What matters is that the process established by those who created the society has been honored.

That process has been honored here. The definition of marriage has been the subject of heated debate in the States. Legislatures have repeatedly taken up the matter on behalf of the People, and 35 States have put the question to the People themselves. In 32 of those 35 States, the People have opted to retain the traditional definition of marriage. Brief for Respondents in No. 14 – 571, pp. 1a – 7a. That petitioners disagree with the result of that process does not make it any less legitimate. Their civil liberty has been vindicated.

B

Aside from undermining the political processes that protect our liberty, the majority's decision threatens the religious liberty our Nation has long sought to protect. The history of religious liberty in our country is familiar: Many of the earliest immigrants to America came seeking freedom to practice their religion without restraint. See McConnell, The Origins and Historical Understanding of Free Exercise of Religion, 103 Harv. L. Rev. 1409, 1422–1425 (1990). When they arrived, they created their own havens for religious practice. Ibid. Many of these havens were initially homogeneous communities with established religions. Ibid. By the 1780's, however, "America was in the wake of a great religious revival" marked by a move toward free exercise of religion. Id., at 1437. Every State save Connecticut adopted protections for religious free *domin* their State Constitutions by 1789, id., at 1455, and, of course, the First Amendment enshrined protection for the free exercise of religion in the U.S. Constitution. But that protection was far from the last word on religious liberty in this country, as the Federal Government and the States have reaffirmed their commitment to religious liberty by codifying protections for religious practice. See, e.g., Religious Freedom Restoration Act of 1993, 107 Stat. 1488, 42 U.S. C. §2000bb et seq.; Conn. Gen. Stat. §52–571b (2015).

Numerous *amici*—even some not supporting the States—have cautioned the Court that its decision here will "have unavoidable and wide-ranging implications for religious liberty." Brief for General Conference of Seventh-Day Adventists et al. as *Amici Curiae* 5. In our society, marriage is not simply a governmental institution; it is a religious institution as well. Id., at 7. Today's decision might change the former, but it cannot change the latter. It appears all but inevitable that the two will come into conflict, particularly as individuals and churches are confronted with demands to participate in and endorse civil marriages between same-sex couples.

The majority appears unmoved by that inevitability. It makes only a weak gesture toward religious liberty in a single paragraph, ante, at 27. And even that gesture indicates a misunderstanding of religious liberty in our Nation's tradition. Religious liberty is about more than just the protection for "religious organizations and persons ... as they seek to teach the principles that are so fulfilling and so central to their lives and faiths." Ibid. Religious liberty is about freedom of action in matters of religion generally, and the scope of that liberty is directly correlated to the civil restraints placed upon religious practice.[48]

Although our Constitution provides some protection against such governmental restrictions on religious practices, the People have long elected to afford broader protections than this Court's constitutional precedents mandate. Had the majority allowed the definition of marriage to be left to the political process—as the Constitution requires—the People could have considered the religious liberty implications of deviating from the traditional definition as part of their deliberative process. Instead, the majority's decision short-circuits that process, with potentially ruinous consequences for religious liberty.

IV

Perhaps recognizing that these cases do not actually involve liberty as it has been understood, the majority goes to great lengths to assert that its decision will advance the "dignity" of same-sex couples. *Ante*, at 3, 13, 26, 28.[49] The flaw in that reasoning, of course, is that the Constitution contains no "dignity" Clause, and even if it did, the government would be incapable of bestowing dignity.

Human dignity has long been understood in this country to be innate. When the Framers proclaimed in the Declaration of Independence that "all men are created equal" and "endowed by their Creator with certain unalienable Rights," they referred to a vision of mankind in which all humans are created in the image of God and therefore of inherent worth. That vision is the foundation upon which this Nation was built.

The corollary of that principle is that human dignity cannot be taken away by the government. Slaves did not lose their dignity (any more than they lost their humanity) because the government allowed them to be enslaved. Those held in internment camps did not lose their dignity because the government confined them. And those denied governmental benefits certainly do not lose their dignity because the government denies them those benefits. The government cannot bestow dignity, and it cannot take it away.

The majority's musings are thus deeply misguided, but at least those musings can have no effect on the dignity of the persons the majority demeans. Its mischaracterization of the arguments presented by the States and their amici can have no effect on the dignity of those litigants. Its rejection of laws preserving the traditional definition of marriage can have no effect on the dignity of the people who voted for them. Its invalidation of those laws can have no effect on the dignity of the people who continue to adhere to the traditional definition of marriage. And its disdain for the understandings of liberty and dignity upon which this Nation was founded can have no effect on the dignity of Americans who continue to believe in them.

* * *

Our Constitution—like the Declaration of Independence before it—was predicated on a simple truth: One's liberty, not to mention one's dignity, was something to be shielded from—not provided by—the State. Today's decision casts that truth aside. In its haste to reach a desired result, the majority misapplies a clause focused on "due process" to afford substantive rights, disregards the most plausible understanding of the "liberty" protected by that clause, and distorts the principles on which this Nation was founded. Its decision will have inestimable consequences for our Constitution and our society. I respectfully dissent.

Beyond Outer Reaches Of Court's Authority

Justice Samuel A Alito

JUSTICE ALITO, with whom JUSTICE SCALIA and JUSTICE THOMAS join, dissenting.

Until the federal courts intervened, the American people were engaged in a debate about whether their States should recognize same-sex marriage.[50] The question in these cases, however, is not what States should do about same-sex marriage but whether the Constitution answers that question for them. It does not. The Constitution leaves that question to be decided by the people of each State.

I

The Constitution says nothing about a right to same-sex marriage, but the Court holds that the term "liberty" in the *Due Process Clause* of the Fourteenth Amendment encompasses this right. Our Nation was founded upon the principle that every person has the unalienable right to liberty, but liberty is a term of many meanings. For classical liberals, it may include economic rights now limited by government regulation. For social democrats, it may include the right to a variety of government benefits. For today's majority, it has a distinctively postmodern meaning.

To prevent five unelected Justices from imposing their personal vision of liberty upon the American people, the Court has held that "liberty" under the Due Process Clause should be understood to protect only those rights that are "'deeply rooted in this Nation's history and tradition.'" *Washington* v. *Glucksberg*, 521 U.S. 701, 720–721 (1997). And it is beyond dispute that the right to same-sex marriage is not among those rights. See *United States* v. *Windsor*, 570 U.S. ___, ___ (2013) (ALITO, J., dissenting) (slip op., at 7). Indeed:

> "In this country, no State permitted same-sex marriage until the Massachusetts Supreme Judicial Court held in 2003 that limiting marriage to opposite-sex couples violated the State Constitution. See Goodridge v. Department of Public Health, 440 Mass. 309, 798 N. E. 2d 941. Nor is the right to same-sex marriage deeply rooted in the traditions of other nations. No country allowed same-sex couples to marry until the Netherlands did so in 2000.
>
> "What [those arguing in favor of a constitutional right to same-sex marriage] seek, therefore, is not the protection of a deeply rooted right but the recognition of a very new right, and they seek this innovation not from a legislative body elected by the people, but from unelected judges. Faced with such a request, judges have cause for both caution and humility." Id., at ___ (slip op., at 7–8) (footnote omitted).

For today's majority, it does not matter that the right to same-sex marriage lacks deep roots or even that it is contrary to long-established tradition. The Justices in the majority claim the authority to confer constitutional protection upon that right simply because they believe that it is fundamental.

II

Attempting to circumvent the problem presented by the newness of the right found in these cases, the majority claims that the issue is the right to equal treatment. Noting that marriage is a fundamental right, the majority argues that a State has no valid reason for denying that right to same-sex couples. This reasoning is dependent upon a particular understanding of the purpose of civil marriage. Although the Court expresses the point in loftier terms, its argument is that the fundamental purpose of marriage is to promote the well-being of those who choose to marry. Marriage provides emotional fulfillment and the promise of support in times of need. And by benefiting persons who choose to wed, marriage indirectly benefits society because persons who live in stable, fulfilling, and supportive relationships make better citizens. It is for these reasons, the argument goes, that States encourage and formalize marriage, confer special benefits on married persons, and also impose some special obligations. This understanding of the States' reasons for recognizing marriage enables the majority to argue that same-sex marriage serves the States' objectives in the same way as opposite-sex marriage.

This understanding of marriage, which focuses almost entirely on the happiness of persons who choose to marry, is shared by many people today, but it is not the traditional one. For millennia, marriage was inextricably linked to the one thing that only an opposite-sex couple can do: procreate.

Adherents to different schools of philosophy use different terms to explain why society should formalize marriage and attach special benefits and obligations to persons who marry. Here, the States defending their adherence to the traditional understanding of marriage have explained their position using the pragmatic vocabulary that characterizes most American political discourse. Their basic argument is that States formalize and promote marriage, unlike other fulfilling human relationships, in order to encourage potentially procreative conduct to take place within a lasting unit that has long been thought to provide the best atmosphere for raising children. They thus argue that there are reasonable secular grounds for restricting marriage to opposite-sex couples.

If this traditional understanding of the purpose of marriage does not ring true to all ears today, that is probably because the tie between marriage and procreation has frayed. Today, for instance, more than 40% of all children in this country are born to unmarried women.[51] This development undoubtedly is both a cause and a result of changes in our society's understanding of marriage.

While, for many, the attributes of marriage in 21st-century America have changed, those States that do not want to recognize same-sex marriage have not yet given up on the traditional understanding. They worry that by officially abandoning the older understanding, they may contribute to marriage's further decay. It is far beyond the outer reaches of this Court's authority to say that a State may not adhere to the understanding of marriage that has long prevailed, not just in this country and others with similar cultural roots, but also in a great variety of countries and cultures all around the globe.

As I wrote in *Windsor*:

"The family is an ancient and universal human institution. Family structure reflects the characteristics of a civilization, and changes in family structure and in the popular understanding of marriage and the family can have profound effects. Past changes in the understanding of marriage—for example, the gradual ascendance of the idea that romantic love is a prerequisite to marriage—have had far-reaching consequences. But the process by which such consequences come about is complex, involving the interaction of numerous factors, and tends to occur over an extended period of time.

"We can expect something similar to take place if same-sex marriage becomes widely accepted. The long-term consequences of this change are not now known and are unlikely to be ascertainable for some time to come. There are those who think that allowing same-sex marriage will seriously undermine the institution of marriage. Others think that recognition of same-sex marriage will fortify a now-shaky institution.

"At present, no one—including social scientists, philosophers, and historians—can predict with any certainty what the long-term ramifications of widespread acceptance of same-sex marriage will be. And judges are certainly not equipped to make such an assessment. The Members of this Court have the authority and the responsibility to interpret and apply the Constitution. Thus, if the Constitution contained a provision guaranteeing the right to marry a person of the same sex, it would be our duty to enforce that right. But the Constitution simply does not speak to the issue of same-sex marriage. In our system of government, ultimate sovereignty rests with the people, and the people have the right to control their own destiny. Any change on a question so fundamental should be made by the people through their elected officials." 570 U.S., at ___ (dissenting opinion) (slip op., at 8–10)(citations and footnotes omitted).

III

Today's decision usurps the constitutional right of the people to decide whether to keep or alter the traditional understanding of marriage. The decision will also have other important consequences.

It will be used to vilify Americans who are unwilling to assent to the new orthodoxy. In the course of its opinion, the majority compares traditional marriage laws to laws that denied equal treatment for African-Americans and women. E.g., ante, at 11–13. The implications of this analogy will be exploited by those who are determined to stamp out every vestige of dissent.

Perhaps recognizing how its reasoning may

be used, the majority attempts, toward the end of its opinion, to reassure those who oppose same-sex marriage that their rights of conscience will be protected. Ante, at 26–27. We will soon see whether this proves to be true. I assume that those who cling to old beliefs will be able to whisper their thoughts in the recesses of their homes, but if they repeat those views in public, they will risk being labeled as bigots and treated as such by governments, employers, and schools.

The system of federalism established by our Constitution provides a way for people with different beliefs to live together in a single nation. If the issue of same-sex marriage had been left to the people of the States, it is likely that some States would recognize same-sex marriage and others would not. It is also possible that some States would tie recognition to protection for conscience rights. The majority today makes that impossible. By imposing its own views on the entire country, the majority facilitates the marginalization of the many Americans who have traditional ideas. Recalling the harsh treatment of gays and lesbians in the past, some may think that turn- about is fair play. But if that sentiment prevails, the Nation will experience bitter and lasting wounds.

Today's decision will also have a fundamental effect on this Court and its ability to uphold the rule of law. If a bare majority of Justices can invent a new right and impose that right on the rest of the country, the only real limit on what future majorities will be able to do is their own sense of what those with political power and cultural influence are willing to tolerate. Even enthusiastic supporters of same-sex marriage should worry about the scope of the power that today's majority claims.

Today's decision shows that decades of attempts to restrain this Court's abuse of its authority have failed. A lesson that some will take from today's decision is that preaching about the proper method of interpreting the Constitution or the virtues of judicial self-restraint and humility cannot compete with the temptation to achieve what is viewed as a noble end by any practicable means. I do not doubt that my colleagues in the majority sincerely see in the Constitution a vision of liberty that happens to coincide with their own. But this sincerity is cause for concern, not comfort. What it evidences is the deep and perhaps irremediable corruption of our legal culture's conception of constitutional interpretation.

Most Americans — understandably — will cheer or lament today's decision because of their views on the issue of same-sex marriage. But all Americans, whatever their thinking on that issue, should worry about what the majority's claim of power portends.

Endnotes

1 http://time.com/3988276/republican-debate-prime-time-transcript-full-text/

2 http://www.apa.org/topics/lgbt/orientation.aspx

3 http://www.csun.edu/~psp/handouts/APA%20on%20Sexual%20Orientation.pdf

4 Draft Petition for Reconsideration and Appendix (addressing Public Health Issues) http://www.usjf.net/obergefell-draft-petition-for-rehearing

5 Draft Petition for Reconsideration and Appendix (addressing Public Health Issues) http://www.usjf.net/obergefell-draft-petition-for-rehearing

6 http://www.cnn.com/TRANSCRIPTS/1502/12/lvab.02.html

7 *Same-Sex Marriage: Efforts To Have Justices Ginsburg and Kagan Recuse Take A Troubling Turn*, by Herbert W. Titus and William J. Olson. https://www.usjf.net/building-the-resistance-to-same-sex-marriage-article-9-recusals-of-justices-ginsburg-and-kagan

8 https://www.law.cornell.edu/uscode/text/5/3331

9 http://www.uscis.gov/us-citizenship/naturalization-test/naturalization-oath-allegiance-united-states-america

10 *Same-Sex Marriage: The Sanctity of an Oath and the Duty to Disregard*, by John Hostettler (https://www.usjf.net/building-the-resistance-to-same-sex-marriage-article-6-the-sanctity-of-an-oath-and-the-duty-to-disregard).

11 *Find the Morality Missing in the Case for Natural Marriage, or Lose,* by Robert R. Reilly (https://www.usjf.net/building-the-resistance-to-same-sex-marriage-article-3-the-missing-morality-argument).

12 *Obergefell v. Hodges: Illegitimate, Unlawful, and a Fraud on the American People*, by Herbert W. Titus and William J. Olson (https://www.usjf.net/building-the-resistance-to-same-sex-marriage-article-14-scotus-decision).

13 *How The Supreme Court Abolished Article V Of The Constitution*, American Spectator, August 15, 2015 (http://spectator.org/articles/63774/how-supreme-court-abolished-article-v-constitution).

14 *The Duty Of Lower Magistrates to Face Down the Tyranny of Same-Sex Marriage,* by Matthew Trewhella (https://www.usjf.net/building-the-resistance-to-same-sex-marriage-article-8-the-duty-of-lower-magistrates).

15 *The Congressional Appropriations Power and Same-Sex "Marriage"*, by Virginia Delegate Bob Marshall

(https://www.usjf.net/building-the-resistance-to-same-sex-marriage-article-12-the-congressional-appropriations-power).

16 Brief for Respondents in No. 14-571, p. 14

17 Accord, Schuette v. BAMN, 572 U.S. ___, ___–___ (2014) (plurality opinion) (slip op., at 15–17).

18 U.S. Const., Art. I, §10.

19 Art. IV, §1.

20 Amdt. 1.

21 Ibid.

22 Amdt. 2.

23 Amdt. 4.

24 Amdt. 10.

25 United States v. *Windsor,* 570 U.S. ___, ___ (2013) (slip op., at 16)(internal quotation marks and citation omitted).

26 Id., at ___ (slip op., at 17).

27 See Town of Greece v. Galloway, 572 U.S. ___, ___–___ (2014) (slip op., at 7–8).

28 Ante, at 10.

29 Ante, at 11.

30 Ibid.

31 Ante, at 10–11.

32 Ante, at 12–18.

33 The predominant attitude of tall-building lawyers with respect to the questions presented in these cases is suggested by the fact that the American Bar Association deemed it in accord with the wishes of its members to file a brief in support of the petitioners. See Brief for American Bar Association as *Amicus Curiae* in Nos. 14–571 and 14– 574, pp. 1–5.

34 See Pew Research Center, America's Changing Religious Landscape 4 (May 12, 2015).

35 *Goodridge* v. *Department of Public Health*, 440 Mass. 309, 798 N. E. 2d 941 (2003).

36 Windsor, 570 U.S., at ___ (ALITO, J., dissenting) (slip op., at 7).

37 If, even as the price to be paid for a fifth vote, I ever joined an opinion for the Court that began: "The Constitution promises liberty to all within its reach, a liberty that includes certain specific rights that allow persons, within a lawful realm, to define and express their identity," I would hide my head in a bag. The Supreme Court of the United States has descended from the disciplined legal reasoning of John Marshall and Joseph Story to the mystical aphorisms of the fortune cookie.

38 Ante, at 13.

39 Ante, at 19.

40 Ibid.

41 The Federalist No. 78, pp. 522, 523 (J. Cooke ed. 1961) (A. Hamilton).

42 The majority states that the right it believes is "part of the liberty promised by the Fourteenth Amendment is derived, too, from that Amendment's guarantee of the equal protection of the laws." Ante, at 19. Despite the "synergy" it finds "between th[ese] two protections," ante, at 20, the majority clearly uses equal protection only to shore up its substantive due process analysis, an analysis both based on an imaginary constitutional protection and revisionist view of our history and tradition.

43 The seeds of this articulation can also be found in Henry Care's influential treatise, English Liberties. First published in America in 1721, it described the "three things, which the Law of England ... principally regards and taketh Care of," as "Life, Liberty and Estate," and described habeas corpus as the means by which one could procure one's "Liberty" from imprisonment. The Habeas Corpus Act, comment., in English Liberties, or the Free-born Subject's Inheritance 185 (H. Care comp. 5th ed. 1721). Though he used the word "Liberties" by itself more broadly, see, e.g., id., at 7, 34, 56, 58, 60, he used "Liberty" in a narrow sense when placed alongside the words "Life" or "Estate," see, e.g., id., at 185, 200.

44 Maryland, North Carolina, and South Carolina adopted the phrase"life, liberty, or property" in provisions otherwise tracking Magna Carta: "That no freeman ought to be taken, or imprisoned, or disseized of his freehold, liberties, or privileges, or outlawed, or exiled, or in any manner destroyed, or deprived of his life, liberty, or property, but by the judgment of his peers, or by the law of the land." Md. Const., Declaration of Rights, Art. XXI (1776), in 3 Federal and State Constitutions, Colonial Charters, and Other Organic Laws 1688 (F. Thorpe ed. 1909); see also S. C. Const., Art. XLI (1778), in 6 id., at 3257; N. C. Const., Declaration of Rights, Art. XII (1776), in 5 id., at 2788. Massachusetts and New Hampshire did the same, albeit with some alterations to Magna Carta's framework: "[N]o subject shall be arrested, imprisoned, despoiled, or deprived of his property, immunities, or privileges, put out of the protection of the law, exiled, or deprived of his life, liberty, or estate, but by the judgment of his peers, or the law of the land." Mass. Const., pt. I, Art. XII (1780), in 3 id., at 1891; see also N. H. Const., pt. I, Art. XV (1784), in 4 id., at 2455.

45 Locke's theories heavily influenced other prominent writers of the 17th and 18th centuries. Blackstone, for one, agreed that "natural liberty consists properly in a power of acting as one thinks fit, without any restraint or control, unless by the law of nature" and described civil liberty as that "which leaves the

subject entire master of his own conduct," except as "restrained by human laws." 1 Blackstone 121–122. And in a "treatise routinely cited by the Founders," Zivotofsky v. Kerry, ante, at 5 (THOMAS, J., concurring in judgment in part and dissenting inpart), Thomas Rutherforth wrote, "By liberty we mean the power,which a man has to act as he thinks fit, where no law restrains him; it may therefore be called a mans right over his own actions." 1 T. Rutherforth, Institutes of Natural Law 146 (1754). Rutherforth explained that "[t]he only restraint, which a mans right over his own actions is originally under, is the obligation of governing himself by the law of nature, and the law of God," and that " [w]hatever right those of our own species may have ... to restrain [those actions] within certain bounds, beyond what the law of nature has prescribed, arises from some after-act of our own, from some consent either express or tacit, by which we have alienated our liberty, or transferred the right of directing our actions from ourselves to them." Id., at 147–148.

46 The suggestion of petitioners and their amici that antimiscegenation laws are akin to laws defining marriage as between one man and one woman is both offensive and inaccurate. "America's earliest laws against interracial sex and marriage were spawned by slavery." P. Pascoe, What Comes Naturally: Miscegenation Law and the Making of Race in America 19 (2009). For instance, Maryland's 1664 law prohibiting marriages between " 'free borne English women' " and " 'Negro Sla[v]es' " was passed as part of the very act that authorized lifelong slavery in the colony. Id., at 19–20. Virginia's antimiscegenation laws likewise were passed in a 1691 resolution entitled "An act for suppressing outlying Slaves." Act of Apr. 1691, Ch. XVI, 3 Va. Stat. 86 (W. Hening ed. 1823) (reprint 1969) (italics deleted). "It was not until the Civil War threw the future of slavery into doubt that lawyers, legislators, and judges began to develop the elaborate justifications that signified the emergence of miscegenation law and made restrictions on interracial marriage the foundation of post-Civil War white supremacy." Pascoe, supra, at 27–28.

Laws defining marriage as between one man and one woman do not share this sordid history. The traditional definition of marriage has prevailed in every society that has recognized marriage throughout history. Brief for Scholars of History and Related Disciplines as Amici Curiae 1. It arose not out of a desire to shore up an invidious institution like slavery, but out of a desire "to increase the likelihood that children will be born and raised in stable and enduring family units by both the mothers and the fathers who brought them into this world." Id., at 8. And it has existed in civilizations containing all manner of views on homosexuality. See Brief for Ryan T. Anderson as Amicus Curiae 11–12 (explaining that several famous ancient Greeks wrote approvingly of the traditional definition of marriage, though same-sex sexual relations were common in Greece at the time).

47 The prohibition extended so far as to forbid even religious ceremonies, thus raising a serious question under the First Amendment's Free Exercise Clause, as at least one *amicus* brief at the time pointed out. Brief for John J. Russell et al. as *Amici Curiae* in Loving v. Virginia, O.T. 1966, No. 395, pp. 12–16.

48 Concerns about threats to religious liberty in this context are not unfounded. During the hey-day of antimiscegenation laws in this country, for instance, Virginia imposed criminal penalties on ministers who performed marriage in violation of those laws, though their religions would have permitted them to perform such ceremonies. Va. Code Ann. §20–60 (1960).

49 The majority also suggests that marriage confers "nobility" on individuals. Ante, at 3. I am unsure what that means. People may choose to marry or not to marry. The decision to do so does not make one person more "noble" than another. And the suggestion that Americans who choose not to marry are inferior to those who decide to enter such relationships is specious.

50 I use the phrase "recognize marriage" as shorthand for issuing marriage licenses and conferring those special benefits and obligations provided under state law for married persons.

51 See, e.g., Dept. of Health and Human Services, Centers for Disease Control and Prevention, National Center for Health Statistics, D. Martin, B. Hamilton, M. Osterman, S. Curtin, & T. Matthews, Births: Final Data for 2013, 64 National Vital Statistics Reports, No. 1, p. 2(Jan. 15, 2015), online at http://www.cdc.gov/nchs/data/nvsr/nvsr64/nvsr64_01.pdf (all Internet materials as visited June 24, 2015, and available in Clerk of Court's case file); cf. Dept. of Health and Human-Services, Centers for Disease Control and Prevention, National Center for Health Statistics (NCHS), S. Ventura, Changing Patterns of Non-martial Childbearing in the United States, NCHS Data Brief, No. 18(May 2009), online at http://www.cdc.gov/nchs/data/databrief/db18.pdf.

About the Authors

Steve Elliott is co-founder and president of Grassfire.com, one of the largest online conservative networks in the country that reaches more than 4 million people each month. Steve brings more than two decades of public policy and communications experience to *Saving Marriage In America.* His written works have sold tens of thousands of copies, and include: *GRIT To Win (2015), High Crimes (2014), Hidden Dangers Of ObamaCare (2013), Thriving In Exile (2012) and The Grassfire Effect (2005).* He holds the M.A. in Public Policy from Regent University. Steve and his wife, Stacy, have five children.

Dr. Herb Titus is a leading authority on the Constitution who has taught constitutional and common law at five ABA-approved law schools over the past 30 years. Formerly an ACLU attorney before his Christian conversion and legal reformation, Dr. Titus has written numerous books, articles and journals.

Notes